Why Lose Weight?

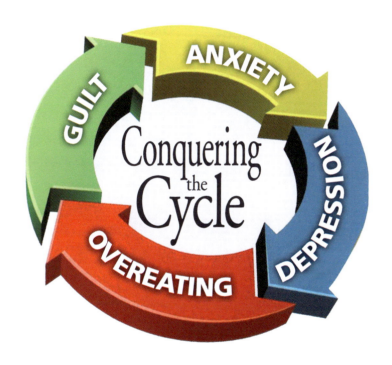

DR A

WILFRED AGUILA M.D., F.A.C.S.

© 2012 Wilfred Aguila, MD
All rights reserved.
Printed in the United States of America.

This publication may not be produced, stored in a retrieval system, or transmitted in whole or in part, in any form or by any means, electronic, mechanical, photocopying, recording or otherwise, without the prior written permission of Wilfred Aguila, MD

Bookmarks Publishing

☙

Weight Success Centers, LLC
Wilfred Aguila, MD
Post Office Box 49009 • Tampa , Florida 33646-9009

Creative Services Group of The Tampa Tribune:
Cover Design and Book Format/Layout by Louise Martin
Chapter Illustrations by Rob Hammons

Charts and Graphs provided by Dr. Wilfred Aguila

Annie Jennings PR
Media Contact For Dr. Aguila
908.281.6201
annie@anniejenningspr.com

Acknowledgements

*Dedicated to my magnificent wife, Sadie.
Without her unconditional love and support
this book would not have been possible*

*And...
to my beautiful children—
Emily, Sarah and Brian.
Thank you for helping me through
my journey and allowing me to
rediscover my life with you.*

*My thanks to
Chandra Moesle Price for editing.*

I developed the information contained in this book about the cycle of obesity over a long period of time. However, the information contained in this book is not intended to replace traditional medical advice from your own doctor. The information contained within this book reflects my personal experience and is provided strictly for educational purposes and general reference.

Similar to every other nutritional, lifestyle, and exercise regimen change, please make sure to consult with your own physician to make sure that change is appropriate for you - this book is not a substitute for medical advice. By purchasing this book you realize and agree that I can provide you with no guarantees – however, this book and its predecessors had a tremendous positive impact on many of my patients. Although claims and testimonials made in this book may not necessarily be typical or average results, everyone is truly different, and I expect that everyone will find some benefit from this book.

By purchasing, following, or reading this book, you also expressly agree to the following terms: I expressly disclaim any guarantees, implied warranties of merchantability or fitness for a particular purpose, and express warranties of any kind – I make none. I expressly disclaim any economic, non-economic, and consequential damages. Further, any and all remedies are limited to replacement of this book. Finally, you agree that any issues or causes of action must be brought in Hillsborough County, Florida.

Publishing/Licensing: Bookmarks Publishing
Author: Wilfred Aguila, MD
Editor: Chandra Moesle Price

Annie Jennings PR
Media Contact For Dr. Aguila
908.281.6201
annie@anniejenningspr.com

"The secret to success is knowing why you failed."

— Dr. Wilfred Aguila

Special Edition - Contains Bonus Chapter

Table of Contents

Preface
    Taking responsibility for myself.
    Helping others conquer the Cycle.

Part 1 – Understanding the Cycle

Chapter 1: Knowing Why You Fail 15
    The battle to keep weight off.
    Changing the way you think about weight loss.

Chapter 2: The Cycle of Obesity 19
    Trapped in a Cycle of Obesity.
    Anxiety sparks stress.
    The development of depression.
    Overeating is the effect, not the cause.
    The feelings of guilt.

Chapter 3: Rotations of the Cycle 25
    Anxiety resulting from abuse.
    Sabotage and friendly fire.
    Daily stressors produce anxiety.

Chapter 4: Controlling Anxiety 31
    Dealing with the anxiety.
    Damage control.

Chapter 5: Understanding Guilt 39
    The pyramid of guilt.
    Overeating during childhood.
    Extreme thinking.
    Immaturity and childish actions.

Chapter 6: Failing to Break the Cycle 47
    Failure is doing nothing at all.
    Consequences of failing to break the Cycle.
    The snowball effect.
    Setbacks are bound to happen.

Chapter 7: The Perfectionist Pattern 59
    Achieving perfection and falling short.
    The role of perfectionism.
    Perfectionists need attainable milestones.

Chapter 8: Psychological Phases of Obesity 67
    Mimicking the classic grieving model.
    Acceptance is your turning point.

Part 2 – Breaking the Cycle

Chapter 9: Don't Choose a Diet, Choose a Transition 77
    No shortage of weight loss tools.
    Build a bridge to a better lifestyle.
    The SIMPLE plan.

Chapter 10: Here's to Your Health 87
    Commit to a healthy lifestyle.
    Repair while you rest.
    Make it a family activity.

Chapter 11: Your Goal is the Secret to Success 97
    Your one and only weight loss goal.
    The importance of moderation.
    Finding a healthy balance.
    Milestones vs. your long-term goal.
    Ingraining healthy habits.
    Training for endurance -- not the sprint.

Chapter 12: Unhealthy Habits and Vices 109
    Exchanging one vice for another.
    Replacing vices with virtues.

Chapter 13: The Real You 113
    Embracing a new outlook on life.

Chapter 14: Conquer the Cycle 115
    Choosing success over failure.

BONUS CHAPTER
Chapter 15: Pulling Out the Root Cause **117**
    Understanding the Seven Root Causes
    Constructing your plan of action
    Finding good OUTLETS
    Plugging into effective OUTLETS

References **130**

Testimonials **131**

Endorsements **132**

Dr. Wilfred Aguila, 2001

Why I Don't LOSE WEIGHT:
Conquering The Cycle Of Obesity

Dr. Wilfred Aguila

Preface...

It was 1991 when I began my surgical residency in Florida. I always wanted to be a doctor, but now I was thrown into a highly stressful training program that required countless nights without sleep and long-hour days. We lived by the motto "eat when you can, and sleep when you can." I can't complain because I received a first-rate training, but I also developed a serious problem with obesity.

I remember one of my instructors taunting me about my weight and betting that I would be over 200 pounds by the time I finished my training. Cruel isn't it, but he was right. I grew to be over 220 pounds by the time I finished. At five feet and seven inches, that gave me a Body Mass Index (BMI) of 34, which is almost a candidate for surgery.

I didn't see myself getting obese. Despite what family and friends said to me, I felt that I looked the same, but I didn't act the same. It wasn't until years later that I finally realized what had happened, and I did something about it.

My journey began on the day that I accepted my obesity problem. Prior to this, I was just in denial. I struggled to find an easy solution to this problem. Multiple diets and books, but not one seemed to offer me an answer. I wanted someone else to do it for me.

Let's face it– we all like food. I had tried all kinds of diets and recipes to lose weight. Most of those recipes did not taste good. The truth is that unless it tastes good - it is not satisfying.

The hardest part for me when I lost weight was the thought of giving up foods that comforted me. All the broiled fish, chicken, steamed vegetables were so Blah. I don't know about you, but if I ate something that was less than appealing, I would not feel satisfied. I then looked for more food to make up for the low levels of endorphins my body was secreting with these low fat/low carb foods. I believe that this is, in part, the reason why we tend to seek other foods late at night or after we eat dinner. I also think that the word diet really stands for "Do. I. Eat. This" rather than standing for a solution to long-term weight loss.

Taking Responsibility for Myself.

There came a time when I finally realized that this is something that I had to do, and no one else could do it for me. I realized that I was going about it all wrong. I was reaching for the wrong goals. It is not the diet that works; it is the understanding of what made me fail and the ability to conquer these issues that made me succeed.

My journey to weight loss began in 2004 and continues even today. Life sometimes throws a curve ball at you, which is why you have to beware of regressing back to old habits. My wife recently suffered a debilitating illness, and I could have easily consoled myself with food. I, however, maintained my healthy lifestyle for my own sake and to maintain the energy needed to take care of her. Because I knew how to spot my triggers, I've been able to stop the Cycle of Obesity and maintain my number one goal to keep the weight off for the rest of my life.

Helping Others Conquer the Cycle.

I titled my book "Why I Don't Lose Weight" because all the other books out there talk about how to lose weight, but not about why you fail. The most important issue to me is how I learned "not to fail." I learned how "not to fail" by identifying my triggers. Once I figured out the triggers, I was able to identify the Cycle of Obesity and determine the means to conquer it.

I have written this book to help others understand the Obesity Cycle. It starts with anxiety, leads to overeating, and then it results in feelings of guilt. This, in turn, leads to more anxiety. Sometimes the Cycle can include depression, which makes the Cycle even worse. Put simply, if we treat only one aspect of the Cycle, say the overeating, then we have not treated the whole Cycle, and you are less likely to succeed. This is why many diets do not work; the whole Cycle of Obesity has to be addressed.

**By controlling our responses to
Anxiety, Depression, and Guilt
in addition to avoiding events of overeating,
we can BREAK the Cycle and can maintain
LONG-TERM WEIGHT LOSS.**

Part I

Understanding the Cycle of Obesity

Chapter 1:
Knowing Why You Fail

The battle to keep weight off.

I struggled with my weight loss for more than a decade. Books, diets, and countless exercise programs did not help until I understood that I was in a Cycle of Obesity. In order to lose weight and keep it off, we must understand obesity. Sounds simple, doesn't it? Obesity, however, is one of the toughest problems to solve. Countless books have been written about obesity, but I believe that to conquer it completely, we have to …

think "outside the box."

This book does exactly that; it shows you how to "think outside the box." I will present many radical ideas about obesity and how to deal with it so that you keep the weight off. This is not a diet book. This is not an exercise book. We will touch on some of these topics, but the real aim of this book is for you to understand obesity and discover the reasons why you fail.

Every other book that deals with weight loss says you should do "this" or you should do "that." Unfortunately, those diet books pigeonhole healthy living into a hobby rather than a way of life. Sure, you may stick with a hobby for a while. Although when you get too busy or are under external stress, time dedicated to your hobby is often the first to be cut from your schedule. That is why weight loss must coincide with a firm commitment to a healthier lifestyle for you and your family. Your health must be front and center. When you focus on taking care of your health first, everything else falls into place, including more time and energy for your family and friends.

Don't shoot for a diet. Your focus should be for a lifestyle change. Remember that you did not gain your weight overnight, and so it will take a while to make the changes necessary to achieve success. Don't be in a rush -- focus instead on a permanent solution.

I personally struggled with weight myself for many years. I felt as if I lost 10 years of my life during the time I was obese. These are years I will never recover or relive, but I can make the most of my future. Losing the weight was as if the clouds were lifted from me.

While you read this, I know you will have many moments where you will say to yourself "oh yeah" or "that makes sense." Take these ideas to heart and apply them. I know that somewhere in this book you will find the reason or reasons that have kept you from keeping your weight off.

I am a Medical Doctor, but I'm writing from a personal standpoint and not from the point of an outside observer or physician. The lessons I have learned and the observations I have made are being passed on to you so that your life will also change. As a bariatric surgeon, I have the privilege of being a surgeon, mentor, life coach, and friend to my patients. I do not take this honor lightly. I have been able to change their lives for the better. That is my life's satisfaction. I've seen patients come through my door with doubt and fear in their hearts. Sadly, this is because so many past programs failed for them. However, with the help of support groups and guidance on how to identify their triggers for failure, my patients have been able to make meaningful lifestyle changes.

Many people have thanked me for helping them with weight loss successes, and their children and families have thanked me for helping prolong the healthy life of their loved one. In conjunction with weight loss, patients have been able to overcome diabetes and other conditions.

Remember, it is life or death for many obese people, which is why it is so important to conquer the Cycle of Obesity. I do not write this book because I think there is one specific tool that will help you lose weight. So many best-selling books, commercial diet programs, and, yes, surgical methods often portray the message that they are the ultimate answer to weight loss. As I tell my own patients, however, success is in the principles and not the tools. While the methods for weight loss vary, the principles are all the same. The core of weight loss struggles is a failure to understand the Cycle of Obesity.

Understanding the Cycle is the blueprint to success in keeping the weight off for good.

Changing the way you think about weight loss.

Life is about finding the right track. You know that you are there because it will feel right. I compare conquering the Cycle of Obesity to surfing. Now I am by no means a surfer, but I have done it a few times. When you surf, you are taught to paddle ahead of the wave until it catches. If you do it right, the wave will catch on to the surfboard. It is like a hook on a conveyor belt catching underneath the surfboard. Once it catches, you move with the wave and take off. When you understand how to conquer the Cycle, it is like catching onto the wave of weight loss.

Most weight loss programs, diets, and interventions have a flaw, and that is you do not change your thinking. The Do I Eat This mentality tends to be severe and extreme, oftentimes requiring you to change everything about the way that you prepare and portion your food, but not your life. This is why diets are so hard to follow, and why we tend to abandon them over time. They reflect nothing about our true lives. This is yet another reason why it's important to forget about the tools and methods, and start thinking about why you don't lose weight.

Chapter 2:
The Cycle of Obesity

Trapped in a Cycle of Obesity.

When I lost weight and kept it off, a thought kept nagging me at the back of my head. I wanted to explain to myself why I got obese in the first place. One day I put these thoughts together and came up with the Cycle that I believe explains obesity. This Cycle is by no means all-inclusive, but I believe it explains most of the causes of obesity and why dieting is not often successful.

If you look closely at the Cycle of Obesity, you will see it explains almost all the situations that affect obesity. The Cycle feeds upon itself and is difficult to break, but break it we must. Long-term weight loss is not possible if only one component of the Cycle of Obesity is treated.

First, it is important to understand how the Cycle works so that you avoid being pulled back into it. You need to identify the pitfalls that will lead you to danger. It is like driving a car. Suppose you are going to take a left turn at a traffic light, but you see an oncoming car. You know that if you don't let the car pass, you are going to be hit. You recognize the impending danger, and you avoid it. The same is true with the Cycle -- you need to recognize the impending dangers so that you avoid getting back into the Cycle.

Of course, you may sometimes be pulled back into a phase of the cycle. Everyone suffers setbacks. Often times, life-altering events can cause setbacks. They typically start with what I refer to as a "foggy period." This is when you don't see anything clearly. Everything seems cloudy and bleak. This period usually only lasts about two days, and then things start to clear up. It is almost like a lens that goes from blurry to in-focus.

As an example of this, let me tell you about my experience in telling patients they have cancer. This is one of the hardest things I had to do as a surgeon.

It literally broke my heart every time I had to do it. I thought of all kinds of ways to soften the pain for my patients, but there wasn't an easy way to do it. The only way was just to tell them the truth. What I found is that as soon as I told them they had cancer, the "foggy period" would begin immediately. They missed everything else I said. I learned very quickly to comfort them and bring them back in two to three days to discuss the options at that time. Invariably, this was enough time to lift the "foggy period" and they were able to see things more clearly then.

Allow yourself the time to get through your foggy period. No matter how bad the setback is, it will ALWAYS clear up in the next few days. If possible, and if it is not going to cause you further harm, temporarily remove from sight any and all things that remind you of your setback. A few days after the foggy period has ended, force yourself to go back to these things. You will see that you will be able to face a situation and approach a plan of action with more resolve.

A plan of action is also key to fighting obesity, and breaking the Cycle is one key to long-term weight loss. Let's go over every aspect of the Cycle in detail. It will make much more sense to you as we go along. There will be "aha" moments, and there will be moments where you may even tear up. Discussing this Cycle with my patients always touches them emotionally in different ways, such as one patient who had a significant amount of guilt she carried due to her father always saying, "You will never amount to anything." This patient began to cry when we discussed the Cycle, and she finally understood the real process that was involved with her obesity. I hope that this Cycle helps you come to terms with your specific issues.

Anxiety sparks stress.

Anxiety affects us all. It is with us on a daily basis. We respond to anxiety with increased stress. Stress takes control, and we then enter the Cycle.

Anxiety in relation to uncertainty represents the fear of the unknown. Such issues as "will I have enough money to pay my bills," or "will I have a job next month" are examples of this. With the ups and downs of the economy and increasing cost of living, it is not difficult to see why fear of the unknown is so prevalent.

Fear affects us all in one way or another. Uncertainty can bring on fear. I have found that many patients with obesity issues fear their friends, family, and even their spouses. The whole gamut of fear may range from the fear of not living up to the expectations of our parents to the fear of losing our spouse or our friends.

The development of depression.

All of us have felt depressed at one time or another. It is a normal aspect of life. Usually, the depression lasts briefly, and we go on with our lives. Depression can be a response to stressful situations. Depression could also be a reaction to not getting what you want. In later chapters, I will go into more detail about this condition. In short, we must learn to differentiate between occasional depression and clinical depression. Clinical depression is much more serious. This type of depression has deep roots and requires professional intervention.

Overeating is the effect, not the cause.

Overeating is a major part of the Cycle, but (contrary to popular belief) it is not the sole cause of weight gain. I will not deny there are people who struggle with overeating and binge eating disorders, but the majority of experts will tell you that episodes of overeating are actually triggered by emotional situations or stress. There are reasons it's called "comfort food." Many say boredom results in their overeating, but from what I've seen in hundreds of patients, that boredom is the result of depression, guilt, or feelings of failure.

As I will discuss in detail later, there are physical mechanisms to prevent overeating, such as portion control methodologies, medications like Meridia, and surgery including the Lap Band®, Roux-en-Y Gastric Bypass, and sleeve gastrostomy. Although I repeat, overeating is not the issue that needs to be examined. The underlying stress or depression needs to be addressed. This is why so many weight loss books and programs have failed to be the secret to success for those struggling with their health.

Many years ago, there were people having their jaws wired shut, and they still found ways to gain weight. They'd slurp milkshakes and pureed junk foods just to satisfy a craving.

My point is that tools and methods for weight loss don't work as a single answer.
You must identify triggers and treat the entire Cycle of Obesity.

The feelings of guilt.

A little bit of guilt is a good check for our actions, but if feelings of guilt go out of control, then this feeds into the Cycle and perpetuates it; thus, this makes it more difficult to change.

My personal struggle with weight loss prompted me to feel guilt on a number of occasions in my life. Of course, I would experience guilt after the act of overeating, but I also felt emotional guilt in conjunction with being overweight. One example pertains to my daughter. I can still hear her voice saying, "Daddy, let's ride the roller coaster together, please!" As I handed my cell phone, eyeglasses, and cap to my wife, my daughter and I headed to the two-seater roller coaster at Universal Studios in Orlando. My daughter and I love roller coasters. I have ridden all types of thrill rides all my life, and now my daughter picked up the same genes. We waited in line and then sat in the car side-by-side. As the lap bar came down, the bar hit my belly and stopped. I tried to take a deep breath and it lowered more, trapping me in an uncomfortable viselike grip, but I did not want to admit to this because I was embarrassed.

Nevertheless, my daughter was practically riding free because the bar did not reach down to her lap. It was going to be, however, a quick ride, and so I held my daughter tight. She held the rails just as tight. I should note that this roller coaster was very safe, and it didn't go upside down or spin around. I felt confident that she would be okay, but her perception of feeling safe, even while I held her down, was not the same.

My daughter acted as if she had a good time, but she did not want to ride the roller coaster the next time we visited the same park. I finally asked my wife what had happened. She admitted that my daughter did not feel safe riding the roller coaster with me because my belly prevented the bar from reaching her lap, and she did not want to tell me so as not to hurt my feelings. In short, my embarrassment for this situation led to a horrible feeling of guilt.

Chapter 3
Rotations of the Cycle

Anxiety resulting from abuse.

There is no easy way to tackle this topic, so I will say it plainly. There is a good amount of mental abuse seen in some patients that are morbidly obese. This abuse may originate in childhood with the parents telling their child that he or she is "good for nothing" or "will never amount to anything." Trying to please parents is a normal behavior for children. When this behavior is met with rejection, the Cycle begins churning. When children feel they cannot please their parents, it does trigger anxiety and guilt in the child. Encouragement is essential to your kids, and it may be the most important intervention to prevent childhood obesity.

My relationship with my father was strained for most of my life. He was a good man, but he was not very encouraging. He would often put me down when I attempted to be creative or show some desire to build something. I spent a great deal of my life trying to impress him. This added to my anxiety, which subsequently created significant guilt. It wasn't until late in his life and prior to his death that he showed me he was proud of my accomplishments.

In addition to parent-to-child relationship issues, sometimes we see mental abuse that originates from the spouses feeling they exert some control over the person by keeping them "fat." When the person loses weight, the spouse feels insecure, and in many cases cannot handle the change. Some degree of jealousy may also be involved. By the way, this spousal abuse may occur as male-to-female as well as female-to-male.

I have seen many divorces take place because of this issue of mental abuse. Eventually, the abused becomes empowered when they lose the weight and then they (in their own words) "throw the bastard out."

"Friends" can also play a role in mental abuse. Yes, it is possible to have "friends" (notice that I put it in quotations) who will hurt you and ignite feelings of fear in you. These people do not say anything about your weight loss, even when you have lost 100 pounds. They do not acknowledge you unless you are failing. Are these really your friends? Good friends will support you and revel in your success. Good friends do not hang around you because "when I am with you I look better."

Sabotage and friendly fire.

Take a moment to think about what I just said about fear and mental abuse. It can be described in one word: sabotage. These people will try to sabotage your efforts to overcome your fears. Many times, they succeed. The anxiety they create is sometimes too much to handle, but it is possible to change it. Again, I am not suggesting that every obese person has this situation. Many people have supportive and nurturing relationships, but the problem I am describing definitely exists … and it exists more commonly than you think. The problem is that many people do not like to talk about it or address it. I am not like other people, this issue needs to be addressed when it exists. If you don't, do not expect good results.

Sadly, sexual and physical abuse may also be involved in the fear aspect of maintaining obesity. The best way to treat this is to allow yourself to lose enough weight to be healthier and to proceed further only when you are comfortable with yourself and have received adequate counseling. It is difficult to start being more noticed. You will absolutely be more noticed and be treated differently when you lose weight. If you are a victim of sexual, physical, or mental abuse, conquering that fear of being noticed will take time and patience.

Victims of sexual abuse may create a safety zone around them by keeping themselves obese. This provides a "comfort zone" in which you believe that nobody will be interested in you and will pay you no attention. In trying to lose weight, you may sabotage yourself unknowingly so that you may keep your safe zone intact. As you succeed in losing weight, you may start to experience a sense of guilt and the anxiety returns; thus, you are thrown back into the Cycle.

The self-sabotage may occur despite your best efforts, and you may be in complete denial of it. For many, feelings of guilt instigate self-sabotage. If you are not comfortable with success, or you don't think you deserve to be happy, you may self-sabotage your own weight loss. Many of my patients have difficulty handling their new look because of their new interactions with other people. They are noticed more. Also, they notice people are more receptive to them. A new world has opened up to them. They believe their personality has changed with their weight loss, and they are not sure how to deal with it.

When I was obese, I avoided the beach altogether. Now mind you, I live in Florida, so it is difficult to ignore the beach. I thought it was because of the heat and the sand. My children love the water and playing in the white sands of Clearwater Beach, but I always made excuses not to take them.

Mrs. ALLTAP

I now realize that the reason for not going to the beach was me. I feared that other people would see me in a bathing suit. They were strangers, so who cares, right? It still bothered me to the point that I would deny my children a fun and normal activity. Now, I have no problem going to the beach with them. It is not my personality that has changed. If I did not really like the beach, I still would not go.

Guess what? Your personality does change with your new look and your weight loss, but it is not a new person you are seeing -- it is truly WHO YOU ARE. Believe it or not, you were a different person when you were obese because many times you were influenced by other factors. You were inhibited in your interactions because of how others perceived you and how you perceived yourself. You likely demand a certain amount of perfectionism in your life, and you feel that others expect it of you.

You are a certain person inside, and this is what comes out when you take control of yourself and stand tall. The "true you" is who you are when you are no longer obese and when you have conquered your FEARS.

Daily stressors produce anxiety.

Anxiety also has other factors including daily stressors such as getting the kids to school, driving them to soccer practice, and getting to work on time. Many of us are trying to be "all things to all people." I have news for you… you can't be all things to all people. Eventually it will collapse. You must have a strong foundation first in order to support the structures above. By this, I mean that you have to take care of yourself first in order to be there for the others. "Sacrificing" oneself for your family is admirable, but what is going to happen to them when they don't have you? I am serious. What will happen to them if you die of heart disease, diabetes, or even cancer because of your obesity? Moreover, what example are you giving to your kids, and will they be obese as well because of this?

I remember one patient who has a family with several kids of different ages and a loving husband. I will call her Mrs. Alltap (ALL Things to All People). Mrs. Alltap was always there for her family. She prepared breakfast, packed lunches, and took the kids to school in the morning. She then went to her 9:00-5:00 job, and then picked the girls up to take them to gymnastics practice and the boy to martial arts. At 7:00 p.m., she drove everyone home and made dinner. Help with showers and homework followed, and the kids were finally in bed. By this time, Mrs. Alltap would sit down in front of the TV to sign all the daily school papers and teacher's notes. Then she would "pass out" on the couch only to get up, go to bed, and start the routine back up the next day.

Mrs. Alltap was everything to all people, and her daily responsibilities left little time for her to take care of herself. Mrs. Alltap, thus, became severely obese and, as a result of this, became diabetic also. She is only in her forties, and when confronted with her deteriorating health, she became concerned she may not be around for her family that so desperately needs her.

Mrs. Alltap subsequently changed her life. It was not an easy process, but she now has enlisted the help of her whole family and has used her time wisely, such as joining in with her son in the martial arts class to exercise with him, rather than sitting around waiting for the class to finish. She involves her whole family in preparing their meals and their lunches for school ahead of time. She carpools with other moms and dads to take the kids to school and to other games and practices. She also has joined a softball league, which she religiously plays in one evening a week. Mrs. Alltap has currently reached her target weight and is keeping it off. Thankfully, she is also no longer diabetic.

Let's face the fact that the woman runs the show in most households. She puts everything together, and when she is ill or unable to do her part, the whole family suffers. The woman can also change things in the household for the better or for worse. If you are Mrs. Alltap, you can set the pattern for your whole family. If you attempt to do everything yourself and allow your family to set this pattern, you have inadvertently created more stress for your family than you have even imagined. You may very well start them in their own Cycle of Obesity. Breaking the Cycle applies to the whole family, not just you. The whole family needs to support you on this.

Chapter 4: Controlling Anxiety

Dealing with the anxiety.

Anxiety is a difficult issue to control, but there are different methods that we can use to keep anxiety down to a controllable level.

Support Groups

There are support groups in every major city for almost every problem that people may encounter. We fear support groups because we remember the ones that we see on TV in which a person must stand up, state their name, and confess to some awful vice or divulge the deepest and darkest secrets of their lives. Nothing is further from the truth. Support groups are made up of people with similar problems to yours, and they are there to support each other. More so, they are there to remind each member that they are not alone in their particular problem. You feel less overwhelmed when you know others have experienced or are experiencing a similar problem to yours and that they are overcoming it.

Don't underestimate the power of a group atmosphere and the benefits you can derive from it. Having the experience of running my own support groups for several years, I can tell you that the group starts in a meeting room, continues in the parking lot, and on the phone amongst the members of the group thereafter. Many good friendships are fostered in these groups. You can find out about support groups, such as Overeaters Anonymous and other programs conducted by hospitals or physicians, via an Internet search for "weight loss support groups" in your area.

Exercise

I cannot begin to tell you how much exercise can contribute to stress reduction. It seems cliché, but exercise absolutely clears the mind and allows you to better face your stress. Exercise does this in several ways. First, by releasing endorphins, which are chemicals in your body that produce a sense of wellbeing. Second, while you are exercising, you can't help but to concentrate on the activity at hand; thus, your mind is distracted for the period of time you are exercising, which means you get a much needed break in your thought pattern so that you may approach your problems from a fresh and new perspective. Third, exercise requires your body to repair itself; thus, it allows you to sleep better at night. You will sleep more soundly. As you will learn later, adequate rest is also essential in combating stress.

Exercise is also an important part of any weight loss program. Exercise is necessary to maintain weight loss, but we must remember that the most important factor for losing weight is to consume fewer calories. We should not trick ourselves into believing that just exercising everyday will make us lose a significant amount of weight. If you exercise for one hour and burn 700 calories, but you are consuming 3000 calories a day, exercise is really not going to help you.

I'll discuss this more in part two, but you'll basically want to

TAKE IT IN STAGES:

Stage I:
Breathing Exercises To Increase Breathing Capacity

Stage II:
Walking 10,000 Steps A Day Using A Pedometer

Stage III:
Muscle Building And Increased Power Walking

Stage IV:
Cardio Exercises Such As Aerobics, Bicycling, And Running

Stage V:
Intense Challenges Such As Triathlons, Ironman – *The Sky Is The Limit.*

Every good exercise program should come with an equally good meal plan. The simpler you make the meal plan, the more likely you are going to follow it; this applies to every aspect of weight loss. Whatever you do, keep it simple so it becomes a lifestyle change and not another diet. Once you have lost significant weight through eating better, then exercise is key in keeping it off. Start slow… and I always recommend a trainer at first so you learn how to do it correctly.

These would be slow, gradual stages working up to your optimum level for good health. You wouldn't attempt to start snow skiing down a huge, dangerous hill without taking any lessons, would you? And of course, always check with your doctor before you start any exercise program or increased regimen.

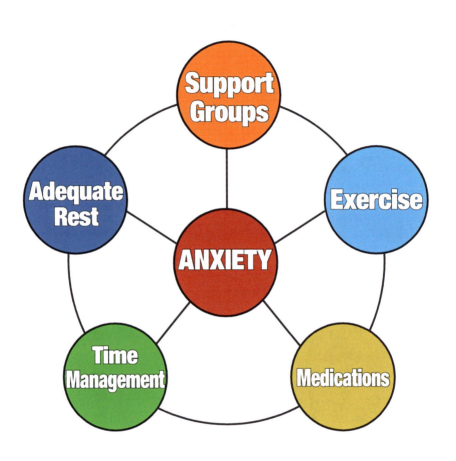

Medications

Sometimes it becomes necessary to use medications to deal with significant anxiety. I firmly believe that medications should be used when other methods fail or when the anxiety is so great, such as the sudden loss of a loved one, that a short course of the proper medications will help in the person getting through this period.

By the same token, medications are given so readily to treat anxiety that other easily applied techniques such as exercise or adequate sleep may be all that was necessary, but were never tried. Again, there is absolutely a place for medications to treat anxiety, and I have prescribed them when necessary because the damage that can occur from not using them is worse for the patient. When it becomes necessary to use medications to treat anxiety for other than short term, then I believe that a psychologist or psychiatrist should also be treating the person. Such issues often require behavioral therapy or other therapy as well.

Time Management

I am not one to talk about this subject because I was often very bad at this, but I learned that I cannot do everything and that I have to prioritize what is most important. That is the key. Prioritize. If you learn anything from this segment, learn that choosing what is crucial, and leaving what is not, will reduce your stress significantly. I know it is hard to decide on what is crucial because at first glance, everything may seem so, but you need to learn to let go.

In surgery training, we learn the term "triage," which means to determine the priority for actions in an emergency. To triage is not easy, and sometimes this action determines who lives or dies depending on the likelihood of survival in (God forbid) a major disaster. It, nevertheless, has to be done for the survival of those who have the greatest need and biggest chance of making it. The same concept applies to our daily lives: We must choose to give our utmost attention to those issues that are essential to our wellbeing and that of our family's wellbeing; in turn, we must leave the other lesser issues for a later time when we may be able to address them better. It can be done. If I can do it, so can you.

Adequate Rest

Sleep recharges the body. During sleep, the body repairs itself and your brain rests. Lack of sleep impairs judgment and makes us less able to deal with stress. We are more likely to feel overwhelmed, and, worst of all, feel more hunger. Our bodies try to overcome the lack of sleep and the fatigue that follows by consuming more calories; this leads into the Cycle of Obesity in the form of overeating. Adults should get at least seven hours of sleep per night, but some may need more. Signs of not getting enough sleep include mood swings, falling asleep at work, in class, or worse in the car. Increased caffeine in the form of coffee (lattes, mochas) or gallons of diet caffeine-laden soft drinks is a common sign of inadequate rest.

I can remember instances in which simply treating a patient with a mild sleeping pill for a short course of time and getting them back in a proper sleep schedule allowed the patient to get back to losing weight again after hitting a plateau.

There is no substitute for adequate sleep.

Eating more and/or consuming more caffeine will not succeed in the long run and will actually cause more harm. Remember the values of regular exercise? Well, here is another instance where exercise is crucial in working out the body to invoke a good night's rest. Healthy living all ties together. It's as if you catch that wave and all things start flowing in the right direction when making healthy lifestyle choices.

Damage Control

Most weight loss experts try to push you to lose weight even when you are facing events that are causing significant stress. By this, I mean more stress than the ordinary day-to-day, like impending loss of a job, potential breakup of the marriage, or behavioral issues with the children such as skipping school or doing drugs.

The point is that these stressors can become rather overwhelming. This is not the time to increase stress. That will only cause you to increase anxiety and worsen the Cycle. It may be best to weather the storm and concentrate only on maintaining your current weight. Maintaining is a victory in itself.

Attempting further weight loss at this time is bound to fail. It is during these instances that we need to go into "Damage Control Mode." What this means is that your current situation is taking up all your thoughts and actions at this time. The Cycle is in full swing, so let's focus all our remaining energy on not causing further damage.

Don't worry about losing more weight at this time because you are not going to be able to do this, and this perceived failure would only increase the guilt in the Cycle and worsen it. Instead, concentrate on not gaining more weight or put all your effort into minimizing the amount of weight you do gain, if any.

I am not suggesting you can eliminate all stress and anxiety. We are adults; as such, we will always have issues of stress. What we can do is control the level of stress and keep it in check so it does not overwhelm us.

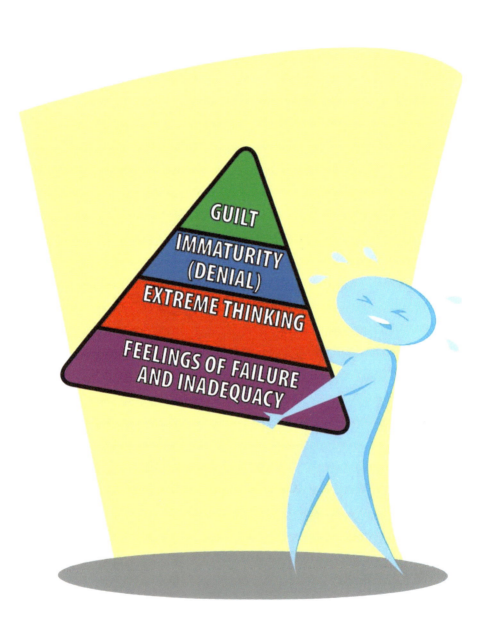

Chapter 5: Understanding Guilt

The pyramid of guilt.

I think of guilt as a pyramid, where guilt is at the top of the pyramid, and the feelings and actions that lead to it make up the base. A little bit of guilt is a good check for our actions, but if feelings of guilt go out of control, then this feeds into the Cycle and perpetuates making it more difficult to change.

At the base of the pyramid are the feelings of failure and inadequacy. This is the belief that everything you try to accomplish is met with failure; this, in turn, makes you feel inadequate. These feelings often lead to the thoughts of "why should I even continue to try" rather than "I need to try harder." Perhaps someone in our lives has made us feel inferior and inadequate by pointing out mostly our failures and shortcomings rather than our successes. We may feel defeated even before we try. Regardless of how it occurred, this is indeed the base of the pyramid, for it supports all the other levels above it.

Feelings of inadequacy may stem from our perception that we are not doing enough or that "things don't get done unless I do them." We feel guilty for allowing time to take care of ourselves. This is very common with mothers who tend to put everyone and everything else first and not leave time to take care of themselves. It is a maternal instinct to take care of your own, but letting your health get away from you will cause further problems that will affect your family in the future.

By failing to manage your weight, complications such as diabetes, hypertension, and even cancer can set in and leave your family without you. This is essentially the situation that you were trying to avoid in the first place. No matter how it hurts, you have to find a way to recruit your family to help. You will be surprised at how much they can. Initially, they will hem and haw, but soon they get used to it and the transition will be smoother. It may feel that you are losing some control over your family, but I am sure they can handle it. They will still love you, and you have not let them down.

It's important to note that those of us who have weight problems often tend to be control freaks. We are really perfectionists at heart, and we cannot let go of guilt. We need to keep it in check or it will eat us up alive. A little bit of guilt is good. It keeps us in control of our actions. If we allow guilt to get out of control, however, it will dominate our lives and leave us with feelings of failure and inadequacy.

My own problems with guilt stemmed from my relationship with my father. We had a sort of strained relationship, and I was not encouraged to succeed. Mostly, I was led to believe that my ideas would not work, and he was not enthusiastic about my success until late in his life. I carried the feelings of failure and inadequacy, and these indeed led me to difficulties with my weight loss among other things.

Guilt imposed on us from our parents is extremely common and is the hardest to overcome. Some parents can make their children feel inadequate, and this fosters feelings of failure. Over time, there is loss of self-confidence, and this is usually life-long.

Overeating during childhood.

If you want to break the Cycle of Obesity, you also have to treat the overeating part of the Cycle. There is a quote from a movie based on the "Red Riding Hood" fairytale, in which Red Riding Hood is anxious and the grandmother is trying to soothe her. The grandmother offers her some porridge and some bread saying, "All sorrows are less with bread."

Sure enough, this is a strategy that is well known by many grandmothers and other assumingly do-gooders. They mean well in trying to soothe your stress with carbohydrates and simple starches– these types of food make you feel good, temporarily, in that they release the proper chemicals in your brain for this to happen. That's the reason they are called "comfort foods." Nevertheless, as said before, a major stress in your life can start the Cycle and trigger overeating, but what also directs the Cycle to the overeating is the OPPORTUNITY. Many of us as children had been conditioned by adults to "soothe our sorrows" with starchy and fatty foods. Well-intentioned family members have repeatedly given us the opportunity, but if we want childhood obesity and later lifetime obesity to be a thing of the past, we need to stop allowing for that first "opportunity" to associate the Cycle with FOOD.

Food is very commonly used to treat stress. Bad news, important decisions, and even ignoring uncomfortable situations are dealt with by eating more. A famous scene in "My Big Fat Greek Wedding" is when Toula is trying to explain to her mother why she is in love with a non-Greek man, and her mother's answer is "Toula, eat something." This is a very funny scene, but it is right on target. This is the way we were brought up to think: the more we eat, the less our sorrows.

We as a society need to start identifying triggers for childhood obesity. We need to educate parents about how to stop the chain of treating anxiety with food, especially early in life.

Through patient interviews, I've identified three consistencies in adults who fell into the Cycle at an early age:

1. Stressful Events
2. Genetic Predisposition
3. And... Opportunity.

Well, we often have no control over a stressful event occurring, such as a divorce or death; however, we can help provide the support and education for properly dealing with life altering situations. Also, we can't change the genetic makeup of someone prone to perfectionist tendencies, but we can educate them on how to harness the power of perfectionistic behaviors, like discipline and endurance, without suffering the downside with self-criticism and unrealistic expectations.

Finally, we may not have the forklifts to remove every candy and soda machine from our child's stomping ground, but we can begin teaching them how to make the best possible choices.

This is just "food" for thought. Whoever is prone to enter the Cycle and use food as the "opportunity" is currently an unknown statistic (perhaps genetics and some degree of perfectionism play into this). Although with almost two-thirds of Americans now overweight or obese, educating parents and making a radical change in how we were brought-up using food for comfort seems well justified.

Additionally, it is not so much how we eat, but when we eat. Take the child who eats a regular-size bag of chips at school for lunch versus the child who gets home and munches on chips all night while doing her homework. Also, the act of eating a big bag of popcorn while watching TV after dinner is very different from eating the single Twinkie at lunch with a sandwich.

Now, don't get me wrong, I am all for healthier food, but remember there is always a starting point. Also, the context in which these foods are eaten is more important than what is being eaten. This is because you are more likely to abuse these "bad food choices" when you associate them with stressful situations or to help control your anxieties. It is, after all, "quantity and not quality."

More calories = obesity.

My point is this: If you want to prevent childhood obesity, you need to worry less about food choices and worry more about when you are eating. Are you teaching your child to associate food with stress and anxiety? To get them "off your back," are you letting them eat at all times? If you do these things, the results can be catastrophic.

Children copy what they see. There are several TV shows now that make binge eating a "gladiator sport," where people eat vast quantities of food while being cheered on by the crowd. Kids can learn this behavior from watching TV, and if they see their parents overeating as well, they mimic this behavior.

The point I am trying to make is that parents **are** the example. Kids may be exposed to all types of behaviors, but they will model what their parents do at home. So don't underestimate the influence you have on your kids.

Similarly, when you are trying to lose weight and you don't include your kids in this lifestyle change, they will inadvertently sabotage and undermine your efforts to eat properly, since they are still eating the wrong things – and you continue to stock the pantry with them.

We tend to blame exercise or lack of activity for the childhood obesity crisis. No doubt that this is part of it. Although remember, kids mimic what we do. If we treat crisis with food, they will do the same. If we encourage them to do so, we will make it even worse.

Teach your kids to eat three meals a day.

Don't let them skip breakfast -- ever. Worry less about what they are eating and more about how much and when they eat it. Very active kids may need a snack, especially when there is a long time between lunch and dinner. Make it a healthy snack (they will get used to eating this way), but by no means encourage them to eat when they are sad, bored, stressed out, or even happy. Don't associate food with emotion, and don't do it yourself because they will likely copy you.

Professor Mark Haub at Kansas State University did a 10-week project in which he ate convenience store foods such as Hostess and Little Debbie Snacks among others, in addition to a protein shake and some vegetables daily. His premise was that it is the amount of calories you consume not the nutritional value of the food that counts. He kept his daily intake of calories to 1800 calories a day. The result was that he lost weight, going from a BMI of 28 (overweight) to 24 (normal weight). In addition, his LDL levels (bad cholesterol) dropped by 20% and his HDL levels (good cholesterol) increased by 20%. His triglycerides went down by 39% (CNN, 2010).

I am not suggesting that you change your diet to Little Debbie Snacks, although they are tasty. The point is we are conducting a "witch hunt" on these foods, when what really matters is changing our old traditional line of thinking of "clean your plate," "remember the starving children," and "here, this will make you feel better."

Let's educate a new generation of parents to understand the undesirable association of food with emotion and the dangers of excessive eating. Let's NOT put our children in the Cycle of Obesity in the first place.

Extreme thinking.

Extreme thinking, or the terminal belief that there is no tomorrow, is thinking only for the now. Little thought goes into the potential consequences. It's as if there is no middle ground. This may occur with many other things in our lives, but nowhere is it more apparent than with food. There is a reckless abandonment when we attack an "all you can eat buffet" or have that dessert even though we cannot eat another bite. Here is where the feelings of failure also play into it: "I am going to have whatever I want today, because I never seem to lose weight anyway-- no matter what I do." Whatever has taught us "we are failures" will continue to reinforce our actions and not allow us to think for the future. It makes us stuck in the NOW mentality.

Remember, setbacks are bound to happen, but they are brief. They last only as long as we allow them to last. Learn to accept the setback and then get things back under your control. Limit the guilt about the set back. Guilt will only perpetuate the Cycle.

Immaturity and childish actions.

There is still one more aspect of the pyramid, and that is immaturity. By immaturity, I mean that we are acting like the child and not the adult who is owning up to our actions. The child wants it now, regardless of what may happen. Never mind that I am already diabetic and have high blood pressure and sleep apnea. Never mind that I have two children and may not be around to see my children grow up or to support my spouse. I am going to do what feels good now because I am going to fail anyway. This is really self-imposed denial. You think, "If I deny it is wrong, it will go away." This is yet another attitude that has a negative long-term effect.

All of these behaviors culminate into GUILT. I believe that looking at guilt in this way allows us to better understand it and, eventually, to keep it in check. Now go back and look at the Obesity Cycle again. Is it starting to make more sense? Does it start to explain a little better why obesity is such a difficult problem to treat? Do you see why a diet or new exercise program alone isn't the answer?

I had a patient who struggled to lose weight, and all it took to change her was a discussion of the Cycle of Obesity and, specifically, the guilt. You cannot identify a problem unless you know it exists and sometimes just arming yourself with this knowledge helps you confront this. It is like "aha," that is what is keeping me from succeeding. Identify your key triggers, and then you can fully understand how to break the Cycle.

Chapter 6:
Failing to Break the Cycle

Failure is doing nothing at all.

What is failure? Failure is NOT re-gaining the weight. Likely, you will have times when you gain some weight or when you "fall off the wagon." This is not a failure. Failure is doing nothing about it. You need to step back and be completely honest with yourself. You need to take a good look at why you failed, and then you need to do something about it. Not doing anything is a complete tragedy -- truly a failure. Just remember: If you don't do something for yourself, no one will. If this sounds cliché, just remember that persistence and determination in time always leads to Success. Stick to it, and it will happen.

Life is about finding the right track. You know that you are there because it will feel right. It goes back to my surfing analogy in the first chapter. When the wave catches your board, you know that you are on it -- there is no doubt. The same happens in your life. When your life catches the right groove or track, you know it; there is no confusing it, but it takes effort to get it. Then, once you are on and riding the wave -- it gets easier to stay on top.

Obesity is likely the biggest fight you will have, but like anything else, you must catch that wave and fight to stay on. You are bound to have feelings before you start, including fear, apprehension, anticipation, or excitement -- these are all natural and expected. The only feeling that you absolutely must not allow yourself to have before you start is the feeling of failure. The one thing that is forbidden is to defeat yourself before you even begin.

Consequences of failing to break the Cycle.

I am not against those people you see on television who are obese and participate in reality shows that give them the confidence to "accept their look" and be happy with the person they are. There is nothing wrong with giving people their self-confidence back; in fact, I encourage it. Nevertheless, I think that there is a very dangerous possibility that we can confuse that acceptance with the idea that obesity is okay.

Cosmetically, obesity may be okay, but medically it is most definitely NOT. We must make this distinction. Obesity carries with it a series of medical conditions that are directly or indirectly associated with it. Most of these conditions are extremely serious and may be life threatening over time. Most of these conditions either improve or resolve with weight loss; therefore, if you accept obesity, you are ignoring the serious health issues that will eventually catch up to you.

Diabetes Type II

By far one of the most common reasons patients come to me for surgery is when they are newly diagnosed with diabetes. The realization they may need to be on medication or even insulin the rest of their lives really frightens them into action. By diabetes, I mean Type II Diabetes and not Juvenile Diabetes. Type II Diabetes is notoriously associated with overweight and obesity. There are numerous studies showing the remission of the disease with significant and sustained weight loss in numbers of about 85% or greater. Numerous studies have found that bariatric surgery can lead to remission of the diabetes in the majority of patients, so much so that there has been a successful push to approve bariatric surgery for people who are mild to moderately obese (BMI 30-34) and not just morbidly obese (BMI 40). The risks of the surgery are considered low compared to the risks of remaining diabetic for the rest of their lives.

What are the risks of being a diabetic? These are multiple. Diabetes occurs when the body no longer recognizes insulin that the pancreas is circulating; the sugars you eat are not allowed to go into the cells where they belong because the insulin is not working. Thus, the "sugars" remain in your blood and create all types of havoc to your body.

The first signs of diabetes can be the need to drink too much water and urinating very frequently. Of course, these symptoms can be from other things such as urinary infection, prostatitis in men, etc., but in an obese person this should be checked to assure it is not from diabetes. Your doctor can do this with a simple blood test called a "hemoglobin A1c." This test will check your blood for the previous few months to see if you have diabetes. A high percentage number suggests that you have it.

High Blood Pressure

High blood pressure or "hypertension" is quite common in obesity and this can lead to multiple problems such as heart disease through hardening of the arteries, stroke, peripheral vascular disease, and even kidney disease requiring dialysis. If you took a toy water-blaster and fired it at a painted wall in your house every day all day long, you will notice that eventually you will chip the paint off the wall and may even cause damage to the structure of the wall. Well, the same thing happens with high blood pressure. The continuous battering of your blood in a pressure jet against the walls of your arteries on a daily basis eventually leads to damage of the lining of the artery and of the wall itself. When this happens, the body fixes it by adding calcium to strengthen the wall and, thus, a plaque is formed. Now the artery narrows even more, and, when this happens, the speed and force of the blood passing through this narrowed area is even faster.

Have you ever put your finger over the nozzle of a garden hose to make the water pressure higher? It's the same concept. As the blood now goes through the narrowed artery at higher speed and pressure, it injures the artery more and an endless cycle is produced.

Because the hardening of the arteries with plaque can occur anywhere in the body, and does, this involves the heart arteries, the brain arteries, and the leg arteries leading to heart attacks, strokes, and vascular disease of the legs. Add to that cigarette smoking, which makes the arteries get smaller and spasm -- and there you have a lethal combination.

In many cases, hypertension is weight related and simply losing weight will either improve or resolve the high blood pressure and get you off the medications. The alternative of leaving the hypertension untreated can be disastrous. Of course, hypertension can be caused by other problems as well: genetics, kidney disease, and rare tumors of the adrenal glands. Obesity, however, remains one of the leading causes.

Because high blood pressure often does not show symptoms at first, you may not be aware that you have it; that is why it has been called "the silent killer." But don't fool yourself. Even if you feel well and have no symptoms, you may still have high blood pressure.

You may be diagnosed with this when you have your blood pressure taken at your doctor's office. Although if you take your blood pressure elsewhere on your own, and it is high, you should have your doctor follow it up at least on two other occasions to be sure that it is hypertension and not due to stress, emotional causes, or other reasons.

Metabolic Syndrome

Simply put, Metabolic Syndrome includes a group of risk factors for heart disease. These include:

- **Abdominal fat or "belly fat"**
  - large amount or predominant amount of fat around the abdomen.
- **Dyslipidemia**
  - high amount of triglycerides and LDL cholesterol, which produce plaque in the arteries.
- **High Blood Pressure**
  - blood pressure equal to or greater than 130/85 mm Hg.
- **Insulin Resistance**
  - the body no longer responds to its own insulin and blood sugar increases; Diabetes Type II ensues.

Metabolic Syndrome leads to plaque buildup in the arteries that affect the heart, brain, and rest of the body, causing heart attacks, stroke, and peripheral artery disease. See how all these diseases fit together to make a cardiac time bomb? If you notice, obesity is at the heart of this. You can see that by losing weight you can improve or resolve all of the above and reduce your risk of a heart attack.

How do you know if you have...

Metabolic Syndrome?

You can measure the waist circumference by using a tape measure just above the hips and measuring around the waist.

- **High Waist Circumference**
  - For men, it's equal to or greater than 40 inches.
  - For women, it's equal or greater than 35 inches.
- **High Triglycerides**
  - Have your doctor order a "lipid panel" and check for .... triglycerides equal to or greater than 150 mg/dl.
- **Reduced HDL or "Good" Cholesterol**
  - For men, it's less than 40 mg/dl.
  - For women, it's less than 50 mg/dl.
- **High Blood Pressure**
  - Equal to or greater than 130/85 mm Hg.
- **Elevated Fasting Blood Sugar**
  - Equal to or greater than 100mg/dl.

Sleep Apnea

Sleep apnea is a disorder in which you stop breathing for short periods of time during sleep. The most common type of sleep apnea is called obstructive sleep apnea in which the walls of the throat collapse with relaxation during sleeping. This type of sleep apnea is most often associated with obesity.

People with sleep apnea may not know they have it, but may be told by their loved ones they snore too loud and even stop breathing. The person with sleep apnea may feel excessive daytime sleepiness, may find it difficult to concentrate, and may feel chronically fatigued. Morning headaches, irritability, and even sexual dysfunction can occur with sleep apnea. Chronic and severe sleep apnea, if left untreated, can lead to heart disease and even death.

The snowball effect.

Here is an example to show how it all ties together. Mr. Sik is a 40-year-old man who is married and has three young children. He is a computer technician working at a local company. He is obese, carries most of his fat in his belly, has a BMI of 45, and is a smoker. Mr. Sik does not exercise (he does not have time), and he skips all meals during the day and eats only when he gets home at night. In the hopes that he will lose weight doing this, Mr. Sik has trained his body not to be hungry at breakfast or lunchtime. When he gets home, he eats dinner and sits in front of the TV or surfs the web on his computer all night. He then goes to bed around midnight and gets up at 6:00 a.m. to start his day again.

Mr. Sik has noted that he wakes up with a nasty headache that lasts most of the morning. He also notices that he is tired and fatigued throughout the day, and he tends to fall asleep at meetings (his co-workers tease him about this). At night, he tosses and turns in his sleep. His wife is constantly complaining about his snoring, and she has noticed that he sometimes stops breathing in his sleep for a few seconds at a time. He doesn't realize that all of these symptoms are due to sleep apnea.

That's not the only issue during sleep. Mr. Sik notices that he drools a lot on the pillows. He sometimes wakes up coughing at night and oftentimes has to take a few Tums to help with his acid indigestion that is "killing him" in the middle of the night. This is due to acid reflux disease, which is quite common in obesity. The excess weight is causing stomach abnormalities including hiatal hernia, which makes it easier for acid to rise up into Mr. Sik's esophagus.

Mr. Sik has opted recently to sleep with several pillows propping him up and has even contemplated sleeping on his recliner instead. He feels that helps him breathe easier. Breathing has been tough since he developed chronic sinusitis. He just can't seem to get rid of his sinus problem despite all kinds of antibiotics and treatments that his doctor put him on. He has also been getting repeated bouts of bronchitis and wheezing for which Mr. Sik has blamed his smoking. Actually, his acid reflux is the culprit. Mr. Sik's acid reflux is causing nighttime aspiration, which has wreaked havoc on his respiratory system.

To keep awake during the day, Mr. Sik drinks lots of diet soda, the more caffeine the better. He drinks diet sodas because he does not want the extra calories. He feels that he needs the caffeine to keep him awake and going throughout the day. There have been days that Mr. Sik has had so much caffeine that he noticed his heart "racing" at times.

Mr. Sik also has noted that he is constantly thirsty and goes to the bathroom to urinate all the time. These are early warnings of diabetes. Throughout the day and especially at night he also feels very "hot." He cranks down the air conditioner, which makes his colleagues and his wife complain. He uses a small portable fan that he aims at himself at his desk in his workstation. He doesn't realize this is due to high blood pressure, also known as hypertension.

Mr. Sik would rather sit, considering that walking is difficult for him. His knees hurt and recently he has noted that his calves hurt if he tries to walk longer than half a block. He notices that if he stops to rest, his calves stop hurting. Mr. Sik even jokes about buying "one of those buggies to get around with."

Mr. Sik cannot bend over or squat down to pick up something because he is unable to catch his breath. He also gets short of breath when he tries to play with his kids. If he exerts himself too much, he notices that he gets some wheezing in his breathing that may take a while to get better once he stops what he was doing. These asthma symptoms are common in obese patients. His legs also swell up all the time, and he has started getting small scabs on his legs that don't heal due to venous insufficiency.

Obesity is also connected to increased estrogen levels. Recently, Mr. Sik has noted that he is not as "romantic" with his wife as he has been in the past. When they try to get "romantic," he seems to have difficulties performing. He has also noted that his breasts appear to be larger and more prominent, sometimes even tender.

He has lost hair on his legs and his skin appears to be dry and cracking most of the time, except at the waistline where he has a chronic rash. The constant skin-to-skin rubbing of his belly rolls has led to a fungal heat rash.

Mr. Sik's story is far too common. Whether you are Mr. Sik or a Ms. Sik, you have likely gone to the doctor to treat these individual symptoms one at a time, when what really should be treated is the Cycle of Obesity. The snowball effect begins with obesity, expands with minor conditions, and grows to include diseases that perpetuate one another. It's imperative that we, as a society, begin looking at the big picture. The Centers for Disease Control (CDC) shows on its website that obesity trends in America are higher than ever, plaguing over a quarter of the population. In order to reverse this trend, we will need to start breaking the Cycle on an individual level. Once the Cycle is broken, you can return to a healthy weight and your conditions and illnesses will likely simultaneously improve.

Setbacks are bound to happen.

As I said before, severely obese people tend to think in all or nothing terms, but there are going to be setbacks when trying to break the Cycle. You need to expect these setbacks and be aware that how you handle these setbacks is most important. If you believe you've been defeated, then you will enter the pyramid of guilt with feelings of "failure and inadequacy." Consequently, this leads into the "all or nothing" thinking. Then you are positioned to enter the Cycle of Obesity again.

Be careful and recognize these feelings. How you address these feelings from the get-go will determine your success. Now at least I have given you a roadmap so that you may visualize how you think and act accordingly. Keep referring back to the Cycle of Obesity, it explains a lot. Use the Cycle all the time, even when you are doing well. It will keep you in check.

Also, keep it in your head that there are two types of sabotage:
    1. Friendly
    2. Unfriendly

The friendly sabotage exists when a family member, spouse, or friend encourages you to do the wrong things only because they are convinced that it is the right thing to do. They do not intentionally mean to hurt you. In family situations or friend situations, when pressured to eat more, show them your "before" pictures. This will remind them why you are doing what you are doing. It will also likely deter the others from overeating. The treatment for the friendly saboteur is education. By teaching them what is correct, you will likely facilitate them to help you.

One of my patients said it best when I explained to her that losing one pound (1 lb.) a week is only 500 calories less a day for seven days. Having realized this, her eyes widened, she smiled and said, "Well, that's a piece of cake." I thought for a moment and realized that it truly is a piece of cake; not in the way that she meant it, but literally. It's one piece of cake less a day, and you have a pound less in a week.

The unfriendly sabotage exists when a family member, spouse, or friend encourages you to do the wrong things in order to make you fail, because this will bring some sort of pleasure or comfort to them. In contrast to friendly sabotage, the treatment for the unfriendly saboteur is elimination. By this, I do not necessarily mean eliminate this person from your life, but sometimes that is what is required considering they may be poisonous to you. This type of problem needs professional counseling (marriage or otherwise). This problem will not go away on its own, and this person will not respond to education. The emotional problems of this saboteur run deep and can even lead to abuse of the person who is trying to lose the weight. Either eliminate the person from your life or eliminate this person's destructive thinking by professional counseling and addressing the behavior head-on.

> *In my office, we have a sign-out desk where we put flyers and brochures. The brochures are usually stacked in order with not one of them falling off the sides. Many times, we disturb the order of the brochures, making sure they are not stacked together but are falling to the sides slightly. This is enough to cause most of our patients to stack them correctly and evenly.*
>
> *The patients don't even realize they are doing it, but they re-establish the order every time. This is part of the perfectionist pattern where everything has to be in order and in control.*

Nowhere is denial more prevalent than with the unfriendly saboteur. We do not want to believe that a person close to us is willing to hurt us, but oftentimes this is exactly what is happening. Deep down in your mind you know it's true; it's just that you have chosen to do nothing about it. Hoping it will go away will not help. For a lot of people, this is likely one of the biggest obstacles affecting their ability to lose the weight and keep it off.

The interactions that you have with an unfriendly saboteur can lead to increasing guilt. This is how the saboteur can control you. It's also how he or she keeps you in the Cycle of Obesity. There is no way that you are going to break the Cycle unless you deal with the source of the guilt.

Sabatoge Flow Chart /Perfectionist Mother

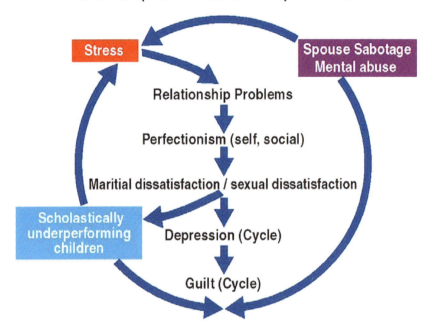

"Individuals who have high levels of self-oriented perfectionism have very high and/or unrealistic goals, expectations, and standards for themselves and place or expose an inordinate importance on sucessfully attaining these standards.

They avoid things that cannot be done well. Socially prescribed perfectinism associated depression and anxiety."

Hewitt and Flett, 1993

Chapter 7:
The Perfectionist Pattern

Achieving perfection and falling short.

One of the most important observations I have made about obesity is that the majority of severely obese people are really perfectionists. This goes against the perceived notion that obese people are lazy or lack motivation. It's quite common to think of obese people as underachievers. Discrimination against obesity is rampant and occurs in the workplace as well as in social situations. It's better to give the job to a thinner more diligent person than the lazy, underachieving, fat person. This is by far not true. Most severely obese people are actually over-achievers and pay great attention to detail, making them excellent workers.

To prove my point, I took the liberty of completing a sampling of my patients regarding perfectionism. Using a Multidimensional Perfectionism Scale (MPS), I took a sampling of 101 patients to examine three levels of perfectionism, including: self-oriented perfectionism, other-oriented perfectionism, and socially prescribed perfectionism.

> *"...you may have self-oriented or self-imposed perfectionism."*

If you believe you can never make mistakes, which is unrealistic given we are all human, you may have self-oriented or self-imposed perfectionism. Growing up with a highly critical parent, or believing you always must meet the highest societal standards, are examples of socially prescribed or perfectionism imposed from others. Although if you are the one demanding that everyone be "perfect" -- you are other-oriented and imposing perfectionism on others.

Out of the sampling of 101 patients, I found that **73% are perfectionists**, which is a large number. Only 27% had no perfectionist tendencies. So roughly, three out of every four patients were perfectionists when compared to the overall community. The community sample, from the MPS, consisted of 1,350 women and 814 men, totaling 2,164 people for comparison purposes (Hewitt & Flett, 2004).

Of the patients who were perfectionists, 60% were one standard deviation or more above the mean, which indicates elevated levels of perfectionism and clinically significant problems. As mentioned, there are three forms of perfectionism: self-oriented, other-oriented, and socially prescribed. Notably, 30% of patients sampled had all three forms of perfectionism. This means they not only expect perfectionism of themselves and feel the pressure of society, but they also expect perfectionism in others. That means their weight loss expert or trainer is also held to a high standard in their eyes. That's bad news if you fall short of their expectations. Failing to keep your promises of quick weight loss will only result in losing their trust.

Self-oriented ranked 12% of the perfectionists, and likewise socially prescribed ranked 12% of the perfectionists. This is significant and goes with my theory that obese people expect perfection of themselves and feel that others expect it of them.

Additionally, 16% of the perfectionists had high levels of both self-oriented perfectionism and socially prescribed perfectionism at the same time, which also goes with my theory that obesity is connected to perfectionism. If they expect perfectionism of themselves and perceive others expect it of them, then setting the bar too high for them will cause them to fail and revert to the Cycle with an all or nothing response. Because they expect us to impose our expectations on them, we need to be careful on what expectations we impose. Coaxing someone along with unrealistic expectations is often the reason why many exercise and weight loss programs fail in my opinion.

So there it is. The majority of obese patients are not lazy procrastinators. They are actually showing above the mean in perfectionist patterns, mostly in the self-prescribed pattern. These numbers were as I suspected because I've personally observed many obese patients with perfectionistic traits.

"The majority of obese patients are not lazy procrastinators."

The struggle between achieving perfectionism and falling short of this is what leads to significant anxiety, and this, in turn, feeds into the Cycle of Obesity. The anxiety eventually leads to guilt because we develop feelings of failure and inadequacy. The guilt and pressure of failure, in turn, leads to overeating.

Severely obese people tend to think in all or nothing terms, which leads to extremes. "If I can't achieve my goals in a self-imposed period of time, then I will just quit altogether." This is not a defeatist attitude as you may think; this is simply not being able to achieve what you perceive as perfection (it is all or nothing).

In addition, the idea that there is a "honeymoon" period to losing weight, after which it is common to gain the weight back, is self-defeating. This idea is a set-up for failure and is a myth. **Your one and only goal is to keep the weight off for good.** If you expect an end to the honeymoon period, you have doomed yourself to fulfill it. Remember that it is not all or nothing. Changing this thought pattern is the hardest thing to do, but it must be addressed in order to conquer the Cycle.

The role of perfectionism.

In my work, if the obese patient is a perfectionist, then you have to learn to use that pattern of behavior to help them. You do this by setting standards and milestones they have to reach and that are realistic enough so they can succeed and do them well, thus, feeding into their perfectionism. This process allows them to feel more in control; therefore, they are more likely to continue. This is why they look for and they need my praises when I see them in the office. Ah ha, they have done something well. The way their faces light up and the pride they feel in what they have accomplished is very noticeable. The opposite is true when they have not achieved success; they act very deflated and pessimistic. Although I don't "yell at them" or make them feel bad for not succeeding, they look for and seek my approval so as to somehow validate their perfectionism.

Many diet experts, exercise trainers, and even physicians do not comprehend this point. They set unattainable goals that serve only to spark the perfectionist tendencies of their clients and patients; in turn, they terminally curb the enthusiasm of the person they are trying to help. Because of the perfectionistic tendencies, obese patients are not well equipped to deal with the standard goals usually set in traditional diet and exercise books. A complete diet change or overly demanding exercise regimen is not always achievable for the long-term – so they fail to stay on the diet or program. The failure they may encounter takes an emotional toll. Remember, self-oriented perfectionism is associated with depression and guilt, which we know feeds the Cycle of Obesity. Perfectionists set their own standards too high, and they expect to do better than what may even be possible.

Often, perfectionists will look to others to help them, and others simply end up helping to facilitate their failure. For example, the gastric band needs to be filled with water in order to give good restriction and make a patient not feel hungry. Although if you tighten the band too much during a fill, the patient may not be able to keep down fluids and process solid foods. In order for the band to work, patients have to eat solid food, which allows them to feel full. Any soft or liquid food tends to go right through the band, never providing a full feeling and leaving you hungry again, within one to two hours after eating.

The fill actually causes more harm than good if the band ends up being too tight because it could encourage the patient to cheat. Patients are only supposed to lose one to two pounds per week post-surgery, which is a proper duration for sustaining a healthy weight loss. However, patients inevitably want a fill. Rather than giving them one, I ask very careful questions to see how they are doing, including: do you feel hungry between meals; are you eating larger portions; and are you always thinking about food? Usually the answer is "No." They don't really need a fill, but their perfectionism is leading them to strive for more, even though what they have accomplished is very good.

Another example is how I see individuals who have high levels of self-oriented perfectionism. They have very high and often unrealistic goals, expectations, and standards for themselves, and they place an extreme importance on attaining those goals. Sadly, this perfection can sometimes lead to dysfunction in relationships and, ultimately, have a negative effect on children. Take for example a perfectionistic and obese mother with a sabotaging spouse who is using mental abuse to control her. These factors promote relationship problems and marital dissatisfaction, which results in depression and guilt (which churns the Cycle). Even worse, the marital dysfunction can ignite stress in their children, which leads to scholastic underperformance and the potential for childhood obesity. In turn, there is further relationship strain and increased depression due to unattainable perfection. One problem just leads to another problem. Perfection is never achieved and the Cycle becomes worse.

Here's one more example. In my office, we see patients who miss their scheduled appointments. We call them and find out why they did not come in. When they finally do return, I find out the reason that they missed the appointment is because they had gained some weight or had been eating the wrong things. They did not want to come in because they were afraid to let me down. We never yell at them or show them disappointment. What the patients really mean is that they have not been able to achieve perfectionism, and they are ashamed of this.

Perfectionists need attainable milestones.

It's important to address your perfectionism if you truly want to conquer the Cycle. The key is to set short and very attainable milestones. Notice that I did not say goals, because the only difficult and long-term target you need to set is the one and only goal of keeping the weight off – for good. The perfectionism can be turned to our advantage to keep every pound that was lost off.

Short and attainable milestones mean that you cannot overload yourself with trying to achieve weight loss as well as making other changes all at once. This is a common mistake by most weight loss experts. It's tough enough to adapt to different eating changes, but when you have to stop smoking, begin exercising, and essentially change your daily rituals all at once, you are bound to fail. This is a big threat to perfectionist tendencies, and this is going to have completely the opposite effect; rather than making a change, it will cause a perfectionist to plunge deeper into the Cycle.

Groups are another way to use perfectionism to our advantage. Groups work because there always is, or at least we always perceive, that there is someone doing worse than you. Sounds bad, but it is human nature. There may be others doing better than you, but it's the ones doing worse who perfectionists also notice. This is why groups work, because they are able to adjust your perfectionism bar (this is not a bad thing).

You see perfectionism has a role. It is key to the understanding of obesity and is the basis by which we can succeed or fail with a weight loss program. Accordingly, the "Extreme Thinking" portion of the Pyramid of Guilt can be replaced with Perfectionism.

Learning to accept less than perfect results will allow you to conquer the guilt portion of the Cycle and lead you one step closer to breaking the Cycle altogether.

Here's one last note regarding obesity being associated with disorganized and cluttered behavior. Quite often, we see a person with a weight problem having a disorganized desk or home. This may not be because they are lazy or dirty. They just might expect a certain level of order and control that, perhaps because of depression or time constraints, they have not been able to address. "If it can't be perfect, then why bother," they think. This all or nothing attitude of being either perfect or being a failure coincides with the negative feelings of failure in the guilt pyramid and churns the Cycle of Obesity.

Chapter 8:
Psychological Phases of Obesity

Mimicking the classic grieving model.

I have made the observation that the phases of obesity resemble the phases of dealing with death and grief. Having been obese myself, I understand that giving up food is like losing a family member or friend who has always been there to comfort us in good times and in bad times. I had to give myself time to grieve the loss of food. We can relate this loss to the well-known model by researcher Dr. Elizabeth Kubler-Ross, which describes the five phases of grieving.[1] Have I shocked you with this statement? Don't be alarmed. Just think about this for a moment.

There are five classic phases of dealing with the death of a loved one or facing the prospect of your own death. The first stage is denial in which the person does not believe that this may be happening to them. The second phase is anger. The person is upset about the particular set of circumstances. The third is the bargaining phase in which the person offers to make deals to avoid the certain fate. Depression is the phase that follows where the person starts to acknowledge what is happening to them and that it is reality. The final stage is acceptance. In this stage, the person understands the situation they are in and accepts it as fact. In this phase, the person affected is more prepared to do something about it. In the case of death and dying, they make plans for the passing away.

The Kubler-Ross model has been applied to any catastrophic personal loss. I believe that coming out of obesity is indeed similar to experiencing a catastrophic personal loss. Food is such a consoling friend to us. As I said before, food becomes such a comfort to us that when we give it up for a diet,

---

[1]The application of Dr. Elisabeth Kubler-Ross's Five Steps to Grief is taken from ON DEATH AND DYING Copyright © 1969. Permission granted by The Barbara Hegenson Agency, Inc. Please visit The Elisabeth Kubler-Ross Foundation's website: www.ekrfoundation.org.

it is like losing a beloved family member or friend. When we have to depart from it, we experience the sequence of grieving I have described. You MUST allow yourself to grieve and go through the following stages in order to reach acceptance and to achieve long-term weight loss.

Denial

Let's look at how the Kubler-Ross model can be related to dealing with obesity. The first stage of obesity I believe is denial. We tend to gain weight and do not even notice it until it is brought to our attention. How many times have you been asked by someone, "Are you adding a few pounds?" Maybe you see a new picture of yourself and then think the following: "My goodness I have really gained some weight."

We tend to discount our weight gain when we are in this phase of obesity, especially when we eat, considering we give no regard to the fact that we can be doing more damage to ourselves. We simply eat like we do and don't even think about it. We are simply in denial. Another example of this is the comment I hear all the time: "I don't know why I am so fat considering that I eat very little." There is no way you can remain obese and "eat very little." You are getting the calories from somewhere, so again this is denial.

Denial is very serious when it comes to weight loss, and it can significantly impede the progress. Many times people attempt weight loss programs and even surgery because their own family members spur them on; however, they are still in denial about their eating problem and are bound to fail because of this. Denial can also come from the spouse not seeing the changes in weight. It is difficult to see a difference in the day-to-day interactions because the change is gradual, but if you look at it, this is a form of denial. The spouse gets used to seeing the obese partner in a certain way and will only notice a change when he or she sees a before picture. This is important because the spouse may later be the target of the anger phase with the obese partner saying, "How did you let me get this way?"

> *"I don't know why I am so fat ...*
> *I eat very little."*

"How did you let me get this way?"

"I am 240 pounds now, but I know I will never be 300 pounds."

Another example of denial is the thought that "I am 240 pounds now, but I know I will never be 300 pounds." Next thing you know is that you are now 300 pounds. These changes can happen sooner than you think. This is also denial.

When my wife was pregnant with our second child, I was severely obese at the time. One of my workmates used to tease me with saying that I was having sympathy for my pregnant wife by trying to look like her with my large belly. I was eating for three people he would say. Problem is that after delivery, my wife lost the weight, but I remained "pregnant." I was in complete denial.

Anger

The next stage is anger. We all experience anger with obesity. This is the "why me" stage. This is the stage in which we ask: "How did I allow myself to get this way?" We may express this anger upon others during this time as we slowly become aware that we have a problem. This is why we may also blame our spouse: "Why did you allow me to get this way?" You may feel that people around you are not helping. Thoughts of conspiracy and sabotage from family members and friends are common here and must be dealt with appropriately. Sometimes these issues may be real, but most of the time they are not and distinguishing between the two is very important. Attempting weight loss at this time I believe is futile.

The anger phase is the time when you need support from family and friends and work through your thoughts. It is important to understand there is no blame to be placed here. The fact you are obese at this time is not your fault, but it is under your control. Someone blaming you for this, or worse, blaming yourself, is counterproductive and will fuel the anger more.

Bargaining

The anger phase will exhaust itself out rather quickly and then head into the bargaining phase, but this is not the type of bargaining that you may think. This phase is marked by multiple diets, oftentimes extreme, which will likely fail. Here we look for the quick fix (the bargaining). You think, "If I just eat lettuce all day or skip meals I will be back on track and everything will be okay." Wrong! This is indeed "bargaining." You are selling a bill of goods to yourself, and you are trying to believe it. You don't yet understand that there are no quick fixes.

Sadly, this is the phase in which many diet and exercise programs get you. Certain quick-fix programs take advantage of you when you're in bargaining mode. You think, "If I just eat this and do that certain exercise, I will have the body I always dreamed of having." When you find that you can't stick with this unrealistic new lifestyle, you quit and then feel like a failure. This often sends you right into depression and into a bigger Cycle of Obesity than before. Often, people end up putting on more weight than they were before they started the quick-fix program. **This why diets can often cause weight gain themselves.**

Depression

Because of the failure that occurs at the bargaining phase, we now enter the depression stage in which we feel that there is no hope. "Every diet I try fails miserably, and I gain all the weight back and then some." We are now in the Cycle of Obesity.

Depression may be a very difficult phase because we may feel overwhelmed with the task of losing the weight. Add to this several failed attempts and now you may feel more comfortable following the dreaded Cycle rather than making any further efforts to succeed.

Depression may require psychological counseling, medication, or both. I believe the depression phase is when we first start to acknowledge that we have a serious problem, but we have not yet accepted we need help to conquer it. The important thing to consider here is that you are not alone.

"... you are not alone."

It is important to seek help now so you don't sink deeper into depression. By help, I mean talk to friends, family, or your spouse. Let them know you have a problem that you cannot control on your own. This is the first step in reaching the acceptance phase.

Acceptance

When you reach this phase, you have decided you have a difficult problem that will require more than a quick fix and that you need the support of your family and/or friends. You know that you have reached this stage because you think to yourself, "I will not live another day like this." You have set your mind to change and, more importantly, you acknowledge that you need the change. You have now realized that you have to change the very "fabric of your life."

Many times people are forced to reach acceptance when faced with a catastrophic illness related to the obesity, such as hypertension or diabetes. The need to change from pills for the diabetes to insulin injection will force the person to face the obesity issue. Sometimes an event like this will force the person through the phases of obesity all at once and very quickly.

The acceptance phase is when you are most receptive to do what it takes to resolve your obesity. This is when support from family, friends, spouse, and especially your physician is most important. Now you are "all ears," but you need to keep in mind that unlike the bargaining phase when you tried a "quick fix," in this phase you are in the right mindset to make the changes for life.

Acceptance is your turning point.

Take advantage of this phase and use it to the full potential. This is when you need to say, "I will not live another day like this."

This is your turning point, don't miss it or it may take a long time to come again.

It is important to note that the phases do not have to occur in sequence and they may even recur in the future. Once more, you may not go through all these phases, but you will definitely experience some of them.

I reached my acceptance phase when I was becoming borderline hypertensive and looking at the possibility of requiring medications for this. I could not breathe easily and could not even bend over without getting short of breath. On one occasion, we went to some friend's house and got into their pool. This was the very first time we had put my son in a pool. He must have been about two years old. I held him at the steps in the shallow area of the pool and my wife snapped a picture of this first event. When I saw the picture a few weeks later (we did not have digital cameras at the time), I was shocked to see myself. I could not believe I looked like that (hello – denial.). I was angry with myself, and I even barked at my wife: "How could you let me get that way, didn't you see it?" She replied, "Well, I didn't see it either." Then I felt that I had to do something about it right away. I can get this weight off in no time if I just watch what I eat and exercise (bargaining and denial).

I quickly realized that I was not going to eat the "healthy" food my wife was making for me, and I was too tired to exercise when I got home from work. The anxiety increased exponentially and so did the guilt (Cycle of Obesity revisited). Feelings of failure and loss of hope took over (depression/guilt).

With the support of my wife, I took a step back and pulled myself together. I have been a successful surgeon for many years. I have put myself through college, and I have worked hard all my life since finishing high school. I should be able to conquer this problem of obesity, and I said to myself: "It took me a while to get here; it is going to take me a while to get out, but this time it is going to be permanent." I knew that I had to do whatever it would take to get to my one and only goal, which is to keep the weight off for good.

Part II

Breaking the Cycle of Obesity

Chapter 9:
Don't Choose a Diet, Choose a Transition

No shortage of weight loss tools.

In breaking the Cycle of Obesity, you must control the overeating part. This is where most diet and exercise plans out there attempt to "cure" your problem with weight. Problem is that if you do not address the rest of the Cycle, you are bound to fail. Another thing is that not one of these methods to control your eating are "one size fits all." Remember that all the diets, medications, exercises, and even surgeries to control your overeating are just TOOLS that you can use to BREAK THE CYCLE. As long as you understand this, you will be successful.

You want to make sure that you use these tools to your advantage. They will not offer you permanent weight loss if you solely depend on one method alone. Some tools are better than others are, but you have to pick the right ones to help you with your problem. How do you do this? Well, it depends on how overweight you are. Picking the right tools is as important as learning how to use them. You wouldn't use a hammer to remove a screw, would you?

There are many powerful tools out there at your disposal. There are, however, some that are not very effective and should be avoided. Some are also risky and should be medically supervised. Here is an overview of some of the weight loss tools out there today.

Diets

There are as many diets out there as there are starfish in the oceans. The most commonly used diets are the VLCD and the LCD.

VLCD...

stands for a "very low calorie diet." This is usually a 500 calorie per day diet or less that is supplemented by vitamins and may be assisted by powerful appetite control medications that often include an amphetamine-like medication or combinations of such. These diets are dangerous if not monitored closely by a physician and should only be used for the short term. If used for long-term, starvation may ensue and the body will burn lean body mass, which includes muscle in addition to its fat reserves. Side effects can include fatigue, dizziness, palpitations, constipation, and diarrhea among others.

LCD...

stands for a "low calorie diet." This is usually a diet that allows 800-1000 calories per day, but it is fewer calories than what someone should be taking in for maintenance. Although these diets may be better tolerated than the VLCD, a physician should still closely monitor them. Significant problems with nutrient and electrolyte imbalances can occur if this diet is not monitored.

Meal Replacements consist of shakes and bars that carry the nutritional value of a full meal and average about 160 calories each. They are supposed to take the place of a meal, thus the name "replacement." Note that they are not meant as a supplement. Meal replacements are used for VLCD or LCD. They may be used in conjunction with appetite suppressant medications or on their own. Meal replacements may also be used in the maintenance phase of weight loss to limit the calories taken at any one meal, say for instance, breakfast. Meal replacements can also include a whole sleuth of commercially prepared and delivered foods that limit the amount of calories you consume per day. These can be very convenient and they relieve the stress of having to prepare your own meals.

Medications

The arsenal of appetite suppressant medications that are FDA approved is very small. No new drugs have been approved by the FDA for the treatment of obesity in over a decade. In fact, as I write this chapter, Meridia was just taken off the market by its maker at the request of the FDA due to recent studies showing significant risks with heart disease and stroke.

Some of the drugs that are on the market are diethylproprion (Tenuate), phentermine (Adipex) and phendimetrazine (Bontril). All of these drugs stimulate the functional activity of the brain that reduce appetite or promote the feeling of satisfaction. The side effects of these drugs can include heart palpitations, increased heart rate, diarrhea, restlessness, and insomnia. All these appetite suppressants are meant to be taken for a short term.

Bupropion (Wellbutryn) works on the serotonin levels of the brain to treat depression and has become a popular anti-depressant for obese and overweight patients. It's parent drug is diethylpropion (Tenuate), which has been used as an appetite suppressant for decades.

Orlistat (Xenical), or over-the-counter Alli, works by binding with the fat that you eat in the intestine and preventing some of the fat from being absorbed, thus reducing the calories. Side effects include oily loose stools.

Keep in mind that all of these drugs are "bridges" to permanent weight loss. They can only buy you time until you, ultimately, **break the Cycle of Obesity.**

Exercise

Exercise by itself is not the best method for long-term weight loss. A good exercise program has to be combined with a well-designed caloric restriction program. What good is burning off 400-500 calories exercising if you are taking in 3000 calories a day?

A good exercise program should be gradual and take into account your limitations. Not all workout programs are the same. One must find a good trainer that is well qualified to help with the journey. A trainer should be meticulous in the way he or she sets up your exercise program. He or she should move you up gradually as you improve endurance and stamina. My trainer, Kaj Gruening, is such a trainer. He focuses very carefully on a whole body approach. There are likely many qualified trainers in your area. BE PICKY and choose the right one; it will pay off in the end because you are more likely to stick with your exercise program if you enjoy it.

For those unable to join a gym or find a personal trainer, there is always the local YMCA. The whole family can pick activities that are suitable for them. The YMCA is affordable and allows you to exercise while your child is practicing basketball or volleyball. Often that's a win-win situation.

Surgery

Gastric Bypass, or Roux-en-Y...

is an operation originated in the 1960's, when patients had a part of their stomachs removed due to ulcers because there were no anti-ulcer medications like the ones today. The observation was made that these patients actually lost weight -- a lot of weight. With some adjustments, the operation was applied to the morbidly obese. The operation is not without its dangers, however, and the early on risks of death with this operation were quite high. With many years of experience and the dedication of many excellent bariatric surgeons, this operation has been improved and modified to where there is now a 1% to 2% mortality rate. Also, it is done by laparoscopy, making the recovery much faster. Because of the bypass segment, certain vitamins and minerals that are absorbed in this part of the intestine will become deficient; therefore, lifelong supplementation of these minerals as well as vitamins B1 and B12 are mandatory. Many long-term studies suggest that the risks from the gastric bypass are more than acceptable compared to the risks of long-term diabetes, hypertension, and heart disease associated with morbid obesity. Potential complications, however, include leak, obstruction, dumping syndrome, ulcers, as well as vitamin and nutritional deficiencies.

The Gastric Band / Lap Band®...

or also known as gastric banding, is a silicone band that is placed laparoscopically on the upper part of the stomach causing a feeling of fullness with less food, about 4-6 ounces of food per meal. The first band was placed in 1978, but it was non-adjustable. The bands did not attain widespread use until the 1990's. That's when technology allowed for the band to become adjustable. It works by causing restriction, and there are no issues with absorption of nutrients because there is no bypass segment. Vitamin B12 injections are not required, but a daily multivitamin is recommended. The gastric bands are adjustable, which allow for steady and progressive weight loss. The mortality rate is lower than the gastric bypass or sleeve gastrectomy, and the gastric band has been shown to be effective in reducing the risks of diabetes and other co-morbidities related to obesity. In fact, the FDA recently approved the Lap Band® for lower BMI's of 30 to 34 with significant co-morbidities such as diabetes and hypertension. Potential complications, however, include slip, erosion, obstruction, and port problems.

Gastric Sleeve...
is a newer operation that essentially removes a portion of the stomach to make it smaller, almost like a tube or banana. Staples are used to divide and close the stomach at its largest side. The operation produces a smaller stomach that is about 25% of its original size and allows for a feeling of restriction; in turn, you eat less. Unlike the gastric bypass, there is no bypass segment of intestine, which results in less nutritional or vitamin deficiencies. Vitamin B12 deficiency is still an issue with this operation because you are removing a portion of the stomach that is necessary for B12 to be absorbed by the diet. The mortality for the sleeve gastrectomy is about 1.4%. Potential complications include leak, infection, obstruction, and severe reflux.

Gastric Plication...
involves "infolding" the larger part of the stomach onto itself with sutures to create a smaller stomach and achieve restriction. Unlike the gastric bypass and the sleeve, a portion of the stomach is NOT removed, so the stomach remains intact. Gastric plications have been used by themselves or in combination with gastric banding to achieve promising early results, but as of yet the current studies are not large enough and this procedure remains investigational.

Build a bridge to a better lifestyle.

We make the mistake of wanting to try all types of diets or methods, but we really don't do anything to change our behavior. We expect a diet to put us on the right course. When you diet, however, you are taking on a behavior that is unreal or deviates drastically from normal human behavior; thus, we do not "stick to it." How can we? Such extreme behavior is not something you can do forever --we are just NOT built that way. Can we really eat a sub sandwich every day for the rest of our lives? Such extreme thinking puts us back into the Cycle of Obesity (remember extreme thinking at the Pyramid of Guilt). If you put yourself on an extreme diet and you cheat, you feel guilty that you cheated. Now you get into the extreme thinking, such as "Well, I messed up today; I will start again tomorrow or next week and do it

right then." You may also think, "I failed again." This also leads you back into the guilt.

The point is you set yourself up to fail in the first place by putting yourself in such an extreme situation that your body cannot possibly handle it or keep it up over a period of time.

This is why you need to think of a diet as a bridge to get you to a better lifestyle. It is NOT a permanent fix; it is only a tool. This is why I say: "Do not choose a diet, choose a transition." If you set up a goal of changing your life and keeping the weight off from the get-go, then you are setting yourself up for success and not failure.

The night of April 14, 1912, the Titanic was crossing the Atlantic on its way to New York when the crew spotted a large iceberg. They maneuvered around it – or so they thought. The iceberg gashed the hull of the reportedly "unsinkable" ship. Within 2½ hours, the Titanic had sunk, taking with it more than 1,500 lives.

What happened? They thought they had maneuvered around it, but while they missed the tip of the iceberg, they struck the massive portion of the iceberg that was underwater. This is what sank the ship.

So let's examine the cycle of obesity again – overeating is the "tip of the iceberg." The massive portion of the iceberg under the water is the rest of the cycle … guilt, depression and anxiety. This is the part we often ignore and, like the iceberg that hit the Titanic, the rest of the cycle of obesity that we don't see, or that we choose to ignore, is the part that is going to sink your ship.

STOP		Take a deep breath and don't panic!
IDENTIFY		Find out which problems or issues are causing you to fail - Root causes.
MANAGE		Resolve to do something about the problems - Find outlets.
PLAN		Create a customized action plan that fits your lifestyle and leads you toward your goals.
LEARN		Gather knowledge from friends and family to help you gain new perspective.
ENVISION		Get a clear picture of the new and improved life you plan to lead.

The SIMPLE plan

It's important to develop a method that is easy to remember. Nobody wants to be a "yo-yo" dieter or someone who repeatedly keeps losing and gaining weight. This is not only unhealthy, but it can also get expensive in terms of wardrobe. To provide a more long-term solution, I have developed the S.I.M.P.L.E. plan. Why make life harder than it needs to be with measuring, counting, and analyzing every detail. I believe that the simpler things are, the more likely that people will commit to following it.

You always need to stop and identify the problem. My main reason for writing this book is to help you identify the problems that are affecting your weight loss. By taking a step back and identifying the issues, you are overcoming the denial of the problems. More importantly, you are one step closer to facing them.

Let me reiterate. Once you have identified the problems, you need to manage them. I explain many different ways to manage these problems throughout this book. Use the following outlined methods to help plan your strategies to succeed. These strategies may require help from others including spouses, family members, friends, and even counselors or other professionals. Do not be afraid to ask. I'm willing to bet that you will be surprised at the number of people happy to help you. This is where you learn your options for unlimited potential, be it walking daily with your neighbor or sharing healthy recipes with a colleague.

Last, envision your change. You have to picture your life changing and, above all, identify the GOAL, which is to "keep the weight off." That's the secret. You need to reset this goal everyday - No Exceptions! Your goal needs to be "maintain my weight loss for the rest of my life"

GOAL:
"... maintain my weight loss for the rest of my life."

Chapter 10: Here's to Your Health

Commit to a healthy lifestyle.

So how do you transition? This is important to your success in weight loss. The keyword is transition. You have to go slow and not change too many things at once. Start by taking in about one-fourth less of food than you normally do. Let your body accommodate to this for a couple of weeks, but really stick to this. You cannot fudge on this step. You truly have to eat about a quarter less food. Many of us are creatures of habit, so you are well aware of how much of something you typically eat. If necessary, use a weight scale if you need to or simply fill three-fourths of your plate with food and leave one quarter out. You can then move the rest of the food on your plate around to fill in the empty space so it does not appear to your eyes that you are eating less.

At this point, do not worry about what you are eating, even if it is very high in calories or fat. Concentrate on eating a little less and not anything else. The rest will come, believe me.

> *You are more likely to modify your lifestyle by doing small changes progressively than by changing many things at once.*

Guess what, with time, your stomach actually shrinks in size, and you will feel fuller with less food. How about that. I bet you didn't think that would happen, but it does. When you try this, you will see for yourself. Make use of this sensation of feeling full faster. This will tell you when to stop eating. Do not push it further. Do not take that extra bite or scoop of ice cream or cake. When you are full, you are full.

Illustration Credit: Rob Hammons

If you ignore this feeling,
you'll end up overeating --then feeling guilty --
then back into the Cycle you go.

Now that you have cut your food daily by about one-fourth for at least a month, start cutting your portions in half. It won't be easy at first, but it will be in time. Give yourself a good month or two doing this. You'll note that this will be a little harder to do than the previous step. Stay on this, and do not quit no matter what. This is the key step. Drink a lot of water and keep yourself busy doing other things. Do not change the quality of your food; you want a corndog, eat one and only one.

The Mouse Card Rule.

The portions that you should be eating at this time should roughly resemble a computer mouse for a medium potato. A tennis ball would be equivalent to ½ cup of pasta or 1 cup of raw vegetables. A deck of cards would be 3 ounces of meat. I always found it difficult to remember these, but you can use this illustration to help you keep a mental picture of the Portion Control Mouse. Whenever you look at a plate just think of this mouse holding a deck of cards and tossing a tennis ball.

Don't worry about exercise yet. If you can walk, do some of that, but don't get into a gym and don't buy a bunch of equipment or workout clothes. Remember that changing too many things at once is bound to fail.

If you smoke, don't try to stop now. Yes, you heard me correctly. It is not that I believe you should not stop smoking; on the contrary, smoking is very detrimental to your health. But to stop smoking is a very difficult undertaking. If you try to do this as you are changing your eating habits, then you are absolutely going to fail at both. Remember, one small step at a time. It likely took you years to become obese, so it will take you some time to get out of it.

There are no quick fixes that
last for the long-term.

It should take you several weeks to be able to eat half of what you used to eat, but if you do it every day, it will get easier until it is routine. Take at least a month if not more to do this step and really develop it into a habit. You will notice that you serve yourself a lot less food than you used to, and you do it without really thinking about it. You will feel fuller faster. If you try to eat more, you will likely feel uncomfortable. Use this discomfort as a hint to let you know that you are done. Whatever you do, do not ignore this hint because if you do, over time, you will stretch your stomach again and increase your capacity for more food, putting you back to the point that you had begun. Guilt will come in, and you will be back into the Cycle.

"...now is the time to make better food choices."

Now that you have cut down your portions, it is time to make wiser food choices. By this, I mean that certain foods may not be as appealing to you as they were before. It's funny how this happens -- but it does. Take advantage of this because now is the time to make better food choices.

By better food choices, I mean foods that are lower in fat and healthier for you. Yes, at this point, we are going to eat better, but now it is easier to do (just trust me). Do not be too extreme with this. Do not start eating tofu and sunflower seeds. I mean start eating more foods that are higher in nutrients, and cut some of the fat out of your diet. Start eating more foods that are fresh and choose less processed foods. Cook things on the grill and avoid frying. Discover the many choices of vegetable and fruits that are available to you. You probably know the difference between food that is good for you and food that is bad for you. Often, too much of the "bad" food will literally make you feel bad.

One of the keys to successful weight loss is to learn how to make better food choices, ALWAYS. Notice that I stressed always and that is because when you bring your guard down, you tend to do it again and again. I repeat, making better food choices does not mean eating salmon steaks every day, although there are ways to make a mean salmon steak. Making better food choices means eating five or six chicken wings instead of 20. Having one hot dog instead of two or three plus nachos with cheese at a football game.

You can still enjoy the things that you like, but you need to be smart about it.

When you make a lifestyle change, this means you now think and act differently all the time. This lifestyle change is what you need to get along in your daily life. It will absolutely be difficult at first, but very soon it becomes second nature. You will notice it takes far less effort to keep it that way. I know this from personal experience. Once you realize this, or have that "aha" moment, you are officially leaving the Cycle of Obesity and setting the course to a new life.

Next, it's time to start exercising. As with the eating habits, you want to start slow and ease your way into further activity. Exercise is a key to keeping your weight off. It also provides a sort of "buffer zone" of about 400-500 calories a day that will keep you safe on those days you eat a little more than you should.

By now, you could have **lost between 20-30 pounds** if you've been eating less and making better food choices. Exercise should be a lot easier now because of the weight loss. You will be surprised at the fact that your joints will hurt less, and you will not be out of breath as easily. More importantly, you will have more energy. It's like when you catch the wave. You will know when you've caught on and will have that forceful push to move forward.

Use this newfound energy to your advantage and start by walking 15-20 minutes briskly at least four times per week. Over the next six weeks, increase the walking to 30 minutes four times per week. This is at a minimum. You may think that this is a lot of exercise, but really all this takes is two hours per week total. Half an hour, four times per week, is two hours; that is not a lot, you can do this. As always, be sure to check with your doctor before you start this or any other exercise program.

"... you can do this."

When you walk, remember you need to walk fast enough so that your heart rate goes up. Slow pace walking and stopping does not cut it. As a rough estimate, you should walk fast enough so that you can still speak to someone walking with you, but you are not so out of breath that you cannot speak. Of course wearing a pulse monitor and pedometer is best, but if you cannot afford a pulse monitor, at least get a pedometer. Pedometers are really cheap, and they help you count the number of steps you take in a day, which should be at least 10,000.

Do not try to overdo the exercise. Joining a gym or buying a lot of exercise equipment is not necessary now; there will be time for that in the future should you want it. **Don't go crazy.** The more extreme you get in this, the less likely you will keep it up. Have fun and work your way up gradually; remember that the goal is LONG-TERM.

You are working on a lifestyle change and not a fad. Also, beware of the "protein shakes" and muscle builders. You are working on burning your fat stores for now and your body is NOT going to use your muscle for fuel at this point, not when it has all this fat to use for fuel instead.

You are working on a lifestyle change and not a fad.

Don't be fooled by people telling you that you need to eat several small meals a day if you are working out. That is fine if you are a training athlete with very little body fat. What will happen if you do this is that you will be taking in a large amount of calories daily, more than you need, and your body will not burn down the fat. Excessive calorie consumption will be stored as fat whether it is from protein, carbohydrates, or fat.

Think of the body as a warehouse storing excess calories as fat.

Think of the body as a warehouse storing excess calories as fat. When the body is confronted with more calories than it can use, it finds a place for it in the warehouse (your body).

If you want to keep the weight off for good, exercise regularly -- No Excuses.

Exercise needs to be put in the category of "something that I have to do each day" rather than the category of something that I should do each day.

Exercise needs to be in the same list as brushing your teeth every day, showering every day, and eating every day. Yes, exercise needs to be in the same list as eating.

Just as eating is a daily <u>necessity</u>, so is <u>exercise.</u>

Repair while you rest.

As I said earlier, your body repairs while you sleep. A good seven to eight hours of sleep sends the right workers and supplies to your warehouse while you sleep. If you don't sleep enough, your body cannot complete healing and assumes there is a lack of workers and supplies in the "warehouse." Therefore, your brain requests more resources, which is why you want to eat more during the day. Typically, we crave carbohydrates at this point (Glucose = workers/supplies).

The trouble is that your body does not really need more workers or supplies; however, the body gets what the body wants. It has supervisors who put in requests for more fat and calories from the food you eat in order to store it for energy. The body can't distinguish from lack of sleep versus lack of nutrients and materials. As a result, you are left with extra workers and supplies that must go somewhere, so you put them in storage until you need them. Because there are more than you really needed, you may never use them. They'll just pile up until you have to create more and more storage space for them. Adding this extra storage space in your body is basically adding fat. Proper sleep and rest is essential to maintaining a healthy weight.

Make it a family activity.

Sure, you can go to the gym or get up early to go running, but sometimes conflicts may get in the way. If you commit to making exercise and physical activity a key part of your lifestyle, you must be creative in working it into everyday life. For example, my wife and I have committed to being active when the kids are active. When my son signed up for martial arts, I signed up for the adult class two doors down from him. When my daughter is at soccer practice in the local park, I'm tossing the football with my son on the sidelines. I see so many parents sitting on the sidelines or sometimes in their car just waiting and doing nothing when they, too, could be getting some physical activity.

One of the best ways for the whole family to get activity is to sign up for a YMCA or local gym membership. It's a way for the whole family to get the unique workout or social activity of their choice. I might go lift weights, while the kids and my wife go for a swim. It not only keeps you healthy, but it keeps you happy and the family connected without a schedule overhaul. Remember, physical activity is not a hobby that you do when you have time -- it's a daily necessity.

Chapter 11:
Your Goal is the Secret to Success

Your one and only weight loss goal.

Why is it that people will quit a weight loss program all of a sudden and do not go back? There are many reasons. One of which is that when they achieve a certain weight, they believe they are done and can let their guard down. They feel a sense of accomplishment and often reward themselves with going back to the same habits that got them into trouble in the first place. Does this make sense? Yes, it actually does. Ask yourself what your personal weight loss goal is. Is it getting to a certain weight? Is it looking and feeling better? Is it getting more energy and not feeling tired all the time? Is it to be able to play with your kids? There lies the problem, for all these "goals" are really not "goals." These are milestones in your journey. These milestones are important and should be celebrated fully, but milestones come and go.

> *Here is the real secret…*
> *your one and only goal needs to be*
> *"maintain my weight loss for the rest of my life."*

I cannot stress this enough. This needs to be engraved into your mind and your thoughts. If you've lost one pound, your new goal is to keep that pound off. It should be posted on your refrigerator. You need to remind yourself of this every day -- yes, EVERY DAY.

Okay, think about this for a moment. If you set a goal for a certain weight, you are more than likely to reach that goal or fall short of it and then decide you are done. When this happens, you are going to let your guard down.

You might exercise less. You might reward yourself by eating a little more or by splurging at family gatherings or on weekends. You say to yourself, "I can eat a little more because I am at my goal, I can afford it." I know this pattern. Been there -- done that.

STOP THINKING OF REWARDS.

If you set your goal to keeping the weight off for the rest of your life, then you always have a goal to strive for; furthermore, if you set this as your goal, all the milestones that you called goals, will happen also. It's inevitable that once you catch the wave, it's easier to move forward. By setting your lifelong weight loss as your ultimate goal, you learn to never give up and avoid a wipeout.

By setting the goal of "keep the weight off" you will meet goal on the days that you wwiegh yourdelf and you didn't gain or lose weight. Instead of seeing this as a failure and increasing your guilt and anxiety, you met you goal.

Also, when your goal is "keep the weight off," you are keeping the same goal that everyone else who does not have a weight problem has to set on a daily basis, otherwise they too will gain weight.

So remember, right at this moment (yes, I mean right now), stop thinking of your weight loss milestones as goals. Set your true one and only goal to be:

"Keep the weight off for the rest of my life."

By doing this, you will succeed.

The importance of moderation.

All weight loss programs, diets, and interventions have a flaw; that flaw is that DIETS do not change your thinking. You need to change only one thing, and that is to stop swinging from one side of the pendulum to the other. That means you have to achieve MODERATION.

I know that is cliché, and you have heard this repeatedly, but the truth is that moderation is what keeps you from gaining weight through the holidays. Moderation is what keeps you from splurging every time you go out to eat. Moderation is what keeps you from overeating and putting your next "diet" off until Monday or some other future date. Moderation is what keeps your weight off.

Whatever tools you need to achieve moderation, use them. Achieving moderation in your thinking and in your eating will last your whole life. Don't underestimate its power. We will all be tempted or encouraged to indulge or splurge from time to time, but if we have learned to achieve moderation, then we will go back to that as our guide.

"...you could end up one of those 'yo-yo' dieters."

One of the most important things to learn is NOT to splurge or indulge until you have conquered MODERATION. Indulging before you are able to control your limits is only going to lead you to one of the extremes: either extreme dieting, or full, unbridled overindulgence (overeating). Only after you have demonstrated repeatedly that you can restrain your eating habits, can you allow times of occasional indulgence. Otherwise, you could end up one of those "yo-yo" dieters. Also, remember that as long as you think "all or nothing," it will be just that. As discussed earlier, extreme thinking will result in failure. We should strive to reach a stable weight and put all of our efforts to stay there, rather than trying to reach a goal that will be next to impossible to maintain.

Remember that moderation is also important in exercise. The "all or nothing" mentality prevails here also. I see people begin exercise programs in which they are exercising every day, seven days a week, and several hours a day. This is bound to fail. Like anything else, when you base your plan on extremes, they will not last. Most people will then quit and do nothing.

In addition, some people are unable to exercise. To think that an obese person who has not exercised in many years will be able to get on a treadmill or do abdominal crunches (much less even get on the floor) is completely naive. People who believe this can be done have either never been severely obese themselves or have no clue.

Like losing weight, everyone must find the midline. Start exercising slowly. In some cases, only 10 minutes a day for several weeks until you get more accustomed to it. There is no hurry. Remember that you are going for "long-term."

Finding a healthy balance.

Exercise is necessary to maintain weight loss, but it is absolutely NOT the primary way to lose weight. For example, if you were to exercise strenuously (and I mean breaking a sweat) for one hour, you will burn about 500 calories. Now to lose one pound you have to burn 3500 calories. At this rate, you would have to exercise seven hours to burn one pound of fat or exercise strenuously one hour a day for seven days.

If you decide to have a healthy smoothie after your one-hour workout, you will be putting back around 200 to 300 calories of your 500 that you worked so hard to burn off. This leaves you with only 200 calories burned per workout, and this is not enough to lose a pound a week. If you consume an extra 1000 or 1500 calories a day in your diet, you will NOT lose a pound a week exercising -- you will actually gain weight.

I am not saying you should not exercise. Exercise is necessary to maintain your weight loss and good for heart health; therefore, starting out with proper techniques and developing a daily routine will allow you to keep the weight off once you have lost your excess weight.

Controlling your calories is the way to lose weight; therefore, there is no hurry to start an intensive exercise program. Work your way into it. Take your time to learn good exercise habits and techniques. Use a trainer or consult a professional so that you learn the proper techniques.

"Controlling your calories is the way to lose weight..."

Some severely obese people should not even start with traditional exercises. If you are severely obese, you may not be even able to breathe correctly to exercise appropriately. In these cases, you should start with breathing exercises. You need to increase your Functional Residual Capacity, referred to in medical communities as "FRC." All this means is that you need to increase the amount of oxygen your body takes in. Being severely obese limits your air intake by limiting the expansion of your lungs. Your oxygen levels are also decreased given the amount of tissue your blood needs to circulate through and the increased need for oxygen these same tissues need.

Check with your physician regarding specific breathing exercises to increase your breathing capacity. After you have achieved this, you can start other physical challenges such as brisk walking and slowly increase from there.

> Check with your physician.

A personal trainer is extremely important after you've graduated past a walking program. You are now ready to develop an exercise routine, and you need to do it right. This is the time to hire a personal trainer, even if it is for a few sessions just so that he or she may teach you the basics. I know that the economy is tight, but this is money well invested. Just because you played sports in high school and think you know exercise techniques does not guarantee you know what is best for your body now. A good trainer will show you how to use the fitness equipment properly and tailor an exercise program specific for your abilities at the time, thus, avoiding injury and overexertion. The trainer can also show you how to use inexpensive home equipment and show you exercise techniques that you can do even without equipment.

In essence, use the trainer wisely. The local YMCA has programs and trainers that are available for the whole family and the programs are often affordable for any budget.

Milestones versus your long-term goal.

Remember, the most important question we must ask ourselves concerning our weight loss is: "What is my goal?" As I've said before, the goal of weight loss is: "Keep the weight off for life." The following typical answers to my question are just milestones: to reach my normal weight, to become healthier, to have more energy to play with my kids, to do the things I am not able to do, or to cure my diabetes and come off my medicines. We should celebrate when we accomplish milestones, but these are not the goal of weight loss.

When we set a goal and reach it, we tend to let down our guard because we feel a sense of accomplishment. We have accomplished what we have set out to do, and there is no further challenge. "I made it; I do not need to try so hard." This is why I say the mentioned goals are not really goals; they are milestones and should be treated as such. If you follow the real goal, then you will succeed in reaching all the milestones as well. Remember that maintaining your normal weight requires lifelong surveillance and effort. Obesity is a chronic disease.

I am sure that you have heard someone tell you to "set realistic goals." This is good advice, but remember that the realistic goal is the long-term one. To keep the weight off for life is certainly realistic. Keeping the weight off actually gets easier with time. For example, more exercise leads to improved sleep, which leads to less cravings during the day and less overeating. The list goes on and on. Lifestyle changes occur over time, but once they are fixed, they become second nature.

"...set realistic goals."

I have had to empty the gastric band on some of my patients after several years. These patients have done very well and are now at a normal weight. For different reasons, their smaller stomach may get some swelling or they may have the flu and have vomiting. I usually empty their band out completely, and we let the stomach rest for about a month. The swelling usually resolves in a few days, and soon they are back to eating normal foods. The observation I have made is that despite their gastric band being open and having no restriction (which means they can eat anything), they gain no weight, or two or three pounds if any weight, by the time I see them a month later. These patients tell me they were not struggling to keep the weight off during that time. They just continued to do what they were doing before.

What this shows is these patients have not just lost weight, but they have completely changed their lifestyles. The gastric band is now just a safety net, but they are flying solo. With the help of support groups, these patients have completely changed their attitudes about food. They are able to maintain their weight loss with or without their gastric band. They also understand that their goal is to keep the weight off. They work at it every day, albeit with much less effort than before because they have broken the Cycle.

You do have to continue to keep the guard up, however. Falling back into bad habits, like any addiction, can and will happen. Nature always takes the path of least resistance. Stress, anxiety, and peer pressure can all take a toll. These must be kept in check, or we risk entering the Cycle of Obesity again. Gaining two to four pounds could happen depending on what's

happening in your life. That kind of weight gain is manageable. You can still stop the Cycle. A greater than five-pound weight gain in one month is not good. I'd have to ask, "What are you doing?" Take the time to rethink your strategy. Getting into a routine of healthy eating and exercise sounds cliché, but it is essential. Most importantly, and this speaks to the heart of those perfectionists, maintaining no weight gain can be seen as a victory. Remember, your number one goal is to keep off any weight that you lose. So… if you are not gaining, you're winning.

Ingraining healthy habits.

Do you seriously think that the people who are not obese do not need to work at this every day? You are wrong if you think that. They make the same efforts subconsciously. They need to exercise and watch what they eat also. It is just that non-obese individuals have these behaviors ingrained in their psyche, and they don't even need to think about it. They just do it. This is where you need to get to, eventually.

When you learned to drive a car, you were very self-conscious of all the traffic lights, the oncoming cars, the lane markings, the path to go to work or home, etc. Now, after driving every day for many years, I bet you don't even think consciously of many of these things. That is not to say you ignore the traffic lights or signs, but you "automatically" stop at a red light, go at a green light, and sometimes autopilot your way to work and back home. This kind of "muscle memory" can be applied to your eating habits.

Just think, you do it now when you eat large quantities of food and down it in five to ten minutes. I bet you don't consciously think of that when you are doing it either. So yes, it can be done in reverse to learn how to chew slower, take smaller bites, and automatically quit when you are full.

My patients have to learn to slow down their eating, chew their food properly, and take smaller bites or they will have problems eating. It takes them a while to do it, but when they finally get it, they start to do it automatically. More so, they start to notice and criticize others around them who are eating too fast and too much. They also start to implement these behaviors for their whole family. Soon, they too are eating better and losing weight. I know that changing these behaviors is not easy, but it can be done. It pays great dividends in the long run.

Train for endurance -- not the sprint.

You have heard of "sweat equity" whereas you need to exercise and sweat it out to achieve weight loss. Well, I believe it is more important to gain behavior equity. This is because changing your eating habits is what will really make you lose weight and keep it off. What good is exercising your brains out if you are going to "pig out" later?

"... it is more important to gain behavior equity."

So often, we think of accomplishing weight loss as a "sprint." We start to run out of the gate hard and fast. We feel that we can take on the world. This time we will get to the finish line and win. Well, first of all, this is NOT a race. You must not train for a sprint but, instead, train for endurance. Endurance, according to the Merriam-Webster dictionary is "the ability to sustain a prolonged stressful effort or activity." The key word here is "prolonged." People who train for a 5K run do so slowly to build endurance so that they can sustain a prolonged performance. They do not start running several miles a day from day one. In fact, many runners, including one of my patients, started off by walking, then running for a few minutes alternating by walking again. Now, they can run several miles easily. This took months of training.

The important point to keep in mind here is that only by prepping for endurance are you going to achieve prolonged results. What seems to be a very difficult if not impossible task, becomes easier and easier. So remember, train for endurance and not the sprint.

Chapter 12:
Unhealthy Habits and Vices

Exchanging one vice for another.

The problem of exchanging one vice for another is common in obesity. The obsessive nature of this population of patients leads to replacing overeating with other habits that may be healthier, but taken in excess may be damaging also. Everyone has heard of weight loss patients who have replaced eating with alcohol abuse, smoking, and even sex. Other potentially good replacements can become unhealthy ones as well. It is unclear why people choose certain vices over other vices, but opportunity could be to blame. The upsurge in readily available high-calorie foods of all kinds certainly creates an easy opportunity to feed an overeating habit.

Take for example the person who obsesses about food and finally is able to curb his or her desire to overeat by replacing it with running for exercise. Instead of running for 30-40 minutes five times a week for health, this person runs two hours a day, seven days a week. Every moment this person has off, he is thinking of running. As you know from the previous chapters discussing perfectionism, this activity has now become an obsession and not a healthy alternative to eating.

Time and time again, I have seen very motivated people start off with a "bang" only to cool off within a few weeks or months. How many of us have bought gym equipment that is sitting at home taking up space and cobwebs? The spider is getting a workout.

I can list many examples like the ones above. The runner is bound to quit eventually because he is doing it in excess. Don't kid yourself, if you do it this way, you will eventually emotionally quit or, even worse, suffer an injury that forces you to quit.

So if you look at the cycle of obesity again and replace overeating with anything else... you see it is really a cycle of addiction. This explains why people gain weight after they quit smoking or why people do drugs or alcohol after they conquer their weight loss... they replaced one vice with another and *never broke the cycle.*

Replacing vices with virtues.

Moderation is key. Frankly, if we knew "moderation," we would not have this problem in the first place. If you base your entire weight loss on running, and at some point you suffer an injury preventing you from the daily run, you are likely to gain the weight back without a holistic approach. Similarly, what if you base your happiness on being rich and you lose your job? Does that mean your mental state suffers, too? Yes.

I offer one answer to becoming more well-rounded so that you don't risk failing. Replace unhealthy habits with several different activities. By this, I mean become creative like getting involved in community events, the local PTA, or by volunteering for your community theater. Find more than one activity that you like, become a Big Brother or Big Sister, become a Rotarian, or coach Little League. It is okay to exercise regularly, but not to excess. The important point is not to choose only one thing -- **choose many**. Change your life entirely, and you will be surprised what it is you have in you.

Running a support group is an honorable endeavor, but this activity, in my opinion, does not count. The reason is that you do not expand your horizons, so to speak, with this. An obesity support group still limits you to what you know. Again, running a support group is a very good thing, but do this along with other things. Don't limit yourself.

If you think doing these things are just "not me," think again. Obese patients who have lived a lifetime repressed by their self-imposed limitations often blossom like a flower when they lose the weight. A whole new world opens up to them. Those who make the most of this new life are the ones who are most likely to keep the weight off for good.

*Change your life entirely,
and you will be
surprised what it is you have in you.*

Chapter 13: The Real You

Embracing a new outlook on life.

There is one final point that I would like to make. The new person that emerges with the weight loss is not a new person at all, it is the real you. Think about that for a minute. The "real you" was always there and was ready to come out. What kept it from happening is the way society viewed you and treated you. This society-imposed view of obesity is what has repressed your psyche and kept you from perhaps fulfilling your potential. So don't be afraid of your new thoughts and actions when you lose your weight. Remember this is the real you who is ready to come out. Losing weight does not give you more confidence -- you give yourself the confidence.

All that I have mentioned above sounds rather different from what you have been taught, doesn't it? Guess what … following the advice above helps to treat the Cycle of Obesity, as anxiety, depression, overeating tendencies, and even guilt are improved.

Take for example the person who has been told by his parents that he or she "will never amount to anything" or the person who has been trying to live up to his or her "more successful" older sister or brother. The guilt that you may carry from this is substantial. Although once you have broken the Cycle, you will have a new outlook on life. You will feel that you can take on the world. This is your time to shine, don't let it pass away. Use this brand new power to accomplish things you never thought that you could, because the truth is you've always had the ability to do it. Guilt, be gone.

If you have always wanted to be more involved with your kids' activities, here is your chance. People are going to look at you differently when you have lost weight. It's time to take advantage of this and set yourself off from the pack. Show them what you can do. Believe me -- they will listen. It is unfortunate that our society looks at us differently when we are obese, but we can use this to our advantage and let it empower us as we change.

Chapter 14:
Conquer the Cycle

Choosing success over failure.

As stated before, acceptance is your turning point. Take advantage of this phase. Use it to the full potential. This is when you need to say, "I will not live another day like this." This is your turning point. Don't miss it, or it may take a long time to come again. It's like catching that wave -- you'll know when it's time. With the right positioning, you can ride that wave towards long-term success.

No longer will you wonder the answer to "Why I Don't Lose Weight." The answer has been laid out for you. Just determine your triggers, understand the Cycle of Obesity, set a S.I.M.P.L.E. plan, and set your number one goal to keep the weight off. No exceptions! Don't say, "I want to lose 20 pounds before my sister's wedding." You must keep the goal set that every pound lost will remain off. Good health and happiness drives your motivation.

By broadening our horizons with new challenges and successes, our anxiety and stress levels decrease, too. Depression also improves, if not resolves. The Cycle is conquerable.

Break the Cycle, conquer obesity, and ride the wave!

Why I Don't LOSE WEIGHT:
Conquering The Cycle of Obesity

BONUS CHAPTER

Chapter 15:

Pulling Out the Root Cause

Getting to the root of weight issues.

While working on a companion book to Why I Don't Lose Weight, I had an epiphany regarding the triggers that make us overeat. These triggers often entice us to eat the things we very well know are wrong. Yes, much has been said about what foods we eat, what exercise we do, and what tempts us to overeat. It's apparent, however, that very little is said about the Root Causes responsible for those triggers.

Now the root causes are not the same as the triggers. As discussed earlier, the triggers that make us eat are anxiety, guilt, and depression. The root causes, on the other hand, are the ones that give us the anxiety, guilt, and depression in the first place.

In losing weight, and keeping it off, we need to treat the triggers. But more importantly, we need to treat the root causes. It is just like trying to pull an undesirable weed in your garden. If you just pull the weed, and you don't remove the roots... it will grow back. If you pull it from the roots, it will be gone for good. The same applies to your root causes, which are the true underlying instigators of why you overeat. You must set an action plan to deal with these for good.

Understanding the Seven Root Causes

So how do you fix the root causes? First, identify which ones apply to you. Even though this may seem complicated, it really isn't. There are about seven root causes I have commonly seen in helping hundreds of people overcome their weight problems.

They include:

> **1. Lack of self-confidence**
>
> **2. Being all things to all people**
>
> **3. Perfectionism**
>
> **4. Fear of Failure**
>
> **5. Toxic relationships**
>
> **6. Job dissatisfaction**
>
> **7. Sexual, physical, mental abuse**

Usually there is only one or sometimes two that apply at one time, but many of these root causes overlap each other. I have listed some of the most common characteristics of each so you can discover which ones apply to you.

Lack of Self Confidence

Lack of self-confidence is one of the most common reasons we use food for comfort; some people use drugs or other substances instead. Lack of self-confidence can be due to an oppressive upbringing. Being constantly told or made to feel that you are not good enough can wear on you.

Perhaps you may have self-confidence issues due to your underlying perfectionism and fear of failure. Lack of self-confidence can also be due to many of the other root causes such as sexual/physical abuse as a child or adult. Remember the abuse is not the physical or sexual part; the abuse is the control that the abuser forces over you mentally. The destruction of your self-esteem is what they are after and gives them the "high" they feel; therefore, your self-confidence is what is affected.

Self-criticism, making excuses, unable to make decisions, fear of change, anger, and blaming yourself and others are a few of the characteristics associated with lack of self-confidence.

Being all things to all people

Do you remember the plight of Mrs. Alltap? Being all things to all people can clearly be a root cause that may also be related to the need to be perfect. It's the belief that if you don't do it, it simply won't be done right. This behavior also is associated with a high degree of guilt and a low self-esteem that compels you to try harder.

Some of the features of being all things to all people are mood swings, chronic fatigue, loss of control, feeling like you are drowning, insomnia, the mentality of "it's not done right unless I do it," and irritability.

Perfectionism

I have dedicated entire chapters and articles to perfectionism because it's more common than we think. I see it in almost every patient, yet we tend to dismiss it. If you think in "all or nothing" terms, you have this perfectionism tendency. The problem is when we don't try to get a handle on it and let it control our lives.

Perfectionism can overlap with other root causes such as feelings of failure and being all things to all people. Some of the warning signs are controlling behavior, negativity, anger, chronic dissatisfaction, judgment of self or others, self-depreciation, and social alienation.

Fear of Failure

Fear of failure is a very common problem. It overlaps with many other root causes such as lack of self-confidence, being all things to all people, and perfectionism. But I feel it is a root cause in and of itself because it may very well be THE Root Cause of all the others I mentioned before it.

Characteristics of someone with a fear of failure include constant worrying, anger, sadness, loss of control, impending doom, self-sabotage, denial, disconnection from reality, and difficulty handling criticism.

Toxic Relationships

A toxic relationship is difficult to handle because the person that you have a relationship with means something to you. Whether you like it or not -- what they say or do influences you significantly, so they can sabotage your efforts directly. They may do this by bringing you food and taking you to fast food places all the time. Or they can indirectly sabotage you by constantly putting you down, disregarding your emotions, and essentially damaging your self-esteem.

Toxic relationships can also occur between you and your kids. If you have a teenager "in with the wrong crowd," taking drugs, committing crimes, or destroying their lives, this is going to place a tremendous amount of stress on you because you care about them deeply and they affect you. In turn, this becomes a toxic relationship that will cause you harm. Of course, I am not saying get rid of the kid, but you need to improve this relationship by whatever means are necessary for the good of both.

Telltale signs of a toxic relationship are mood swings, irritability, anger, self-blame, withdrawing from others, feeling numb, fatigue, aches, insomnia, difficulty concentrating, lack of trust in others, disrespect by the partner, and sabotage from the partner.

Job Dissatisfaction

Job dissatisfaction runs the gamut from fear of losing your job to being in a job that takes up all of your time and leaves no time for yourself and your loved ones. You may also have a toxic working environment putting you at a high state of stress. A very demanding boss can do this also. Now add to that sabotage from coworkers who would like to see you fail your diet, and you'll have the "perfect storm."

Signs of job dissatisfaction may include difficulty waking up to go to work, feeling unable to disconnect when not at work, eating all day at your workstation, having no time for yourself, heartburn and reflux, feeling overwhelmed, difficulty sleeping at night, mood swings, irritability, loss of control, and never spending time with family or loved ones.

Sexual, Physical, Mental Abuse

All types of childhood abuse may manifest themselves when you are an adult. The problem is compounded by the fact you may be in denial or do not recall that abuse did happen.

What attracts the abuser is the power or control over the other person. The net effect is to lower your self-esteem and deplete your self-confidence. This severe erosion of your self- esteem is long term and will eventually challenge your attempts at weight loss and in life.

It is estimated that 30 to 40 percent of people with severe weight problems have suffered some form of abuse. I believe that number may be even higher when considering many cases go unreported. So this is indeed an important Root Cause.

Abuse may also be due to mental abuse. A spouse or loved one may want to control you by "keeping you fat," not because they feel insecure about their own looks, but because they think as long as you're "fat," you'll feel insecure about yourself. When your self-esteem is lowered, they have power over you.

Some of the signs of abuse include being withdrawn and shy, avoiding social situations, avoiding eye contact with people, extreme self-consciousness, poor hygiene or grooming, intolerance to intimacy, sexual dysfunction, self-injury, insomnia, anger, and suicidal thoughts or attempts among others.

Constructing your plan of action

Root causes require a long-term action plan to fix them, so it will take some time to change these. That is okay. Remember these root causes took years to develop. Considering they are absolutely the reason you are struggling with your weight, it pays great dividends to be patient and take your time identifying and defeating them.

In my follow-up book to *Why I Don't Lose Weight*, I discuss the seven stages of successful weight loss. In that book, I'm helping people create an Action Plan to include all the necessary methods that will resolve each particular root cause. A carefully constructed action plan allows individuals to break the root causes and maintain weight loss for good.

I have carefully crafted action plans that have been successful time and time again with my patients. Some of the action plans require professional counseling and others do not. If, however, at any time you feel you are in a severe and chronic depression or you are contemplating suicide – you MUST seek emergent professional assistance.

Remember all action plans take a while to work their magic. They are NOT a quick fix, and they are meant to to keep the weight off. The one and only goal is to keep the weight off for good.

Finding good OUTLETS

We now know the triggers are the way we express the root causes, and my companion book offers detailed action plans for treating root causes (which ultimately eliminates the triggers). In the meantime, however, you have to do something about the triggers. So here's my advice for combatting the triggers with OUTLETS.

OUTLETS are Opportunities yoU Take to Lift your Emotional ThoughtS. What do I mean by "opportunities" you take? They are actions you can take to feel better. There are activities you can do to release "feel good hormones" in the brain that are similar to the ones let loose when you eat sweets, carbs, and fats. During certain healthy activities, dopamine and serotonin can be released in the brain just like they'd be released with eating. If you do it right, you will get a similar high and feel just as good.

Here's the trick… these activities have to involve your intellect and your creativity. What this means is they cannot be mindless activities like sitting there, watching TV, or posting on Facebook. The activities need to engage you with creativity, which increases serotonin levels in the brain. The more creative -- like writing a book, picking up a hobby, walking with friends, coaching little league, or joining a softball team -- then the more likely it will serve as an OUTLET.

Don't think this works? Think again. It works amazingly well. Try it and see. The trick is to stick with them and do more than one. The more outlets you plug into, the more energy produced. Your stress level lowers tremendously and your cravings will decrease, too. I promise, but you have to do it.

As you use these outlets and you succeed in them, you start to feel less like a failure. Your guilt level also begins to go down (remember feelings of failure are at the base of the Pyramid of Guilt). As you succeed in these outlets and your feelings of failure go down, your guilt will decrease. You are beating the Cycle of Obesity on more than one front: the guilt and the anxiety.

Plugging into effective OUTLETS

So choose your OUTLETS carefully and pick only the things YOU like to do (this is key). Avoid sedentary activities such as bridge club, poker night, etc. because these activities are conducive to eating. Most sit down activities may deteriorate into eating activities.

So stand and disband. Here is a list of common OUTLETS, but feel free to be creative. If you have a really great one, email me so I can post it. Together we can help others with it.

1. Take a daily 30-minute walk with a friend or family member.
2. Play a musical instrument, even if you are not good at it. Just for you.
3. Coach little league or YMCA soccer, basketball, or volleyball -- whatever you like.
4. Teach other people what you know. If you are handy with computers, for example, volunteer time to teach seniors how to email, text, and enjoy the Web with their families.
5. Join a community club or act in Community Theater.
6. Create something with your hands.
7. Join a softball team.
8. Become a big brother or big sister.
9. Lead a Cub Scout or Girl Scout troop.
10. Get a pet that you have to interact with and have to take outside regularly. This does two things: 1. It gets you out. 2. It forces you to interact with another living thing that, in this case, will not pass judgment on you or threaten you. This will increase your self-esteem. Caution: if you live

alone or you're an empty nester, a pet is a good choice. If you take care of kids in a busy house, this may ADD to your stress and may not be good for you.
11. Join a sailing, driving, or running group.
12. Exercise. Pick something you enjoy – like dancing, swimming, or a favorite sport.
13. Start your own column in a local newspaper.
14. Volunteer at the local YMCA.
15. Lead a support group.
16. Throw the ball with your kids daily.
17. Drive cancer patients to and from their doctor's visits or chemotherapy treatments.
18. Join the Elks, Rotary, Four H, Freemasons, or a group where you can make a difference.
19. Start knitting or learn crochet.
20. Take a night class.
21. Take a Martial Arts class.
22. Join and contribute to a book club.
23. Renew your faith.
24. Get involved in your church groups or other organizations.
25. Use your energy and perfectionism to make a difference in others' lives, which will absolutely empower you to feel better about yourself and will increase your self-confidence.

Whatever you do to empower others will pay you back in "spades" by increasing your self-confidence and building up your self-esteem.

Remember... You Matter.

Another Success Story

Jennifer lost **200** pounds!

Another Success Story

Mike
lost **170** pounds!

before

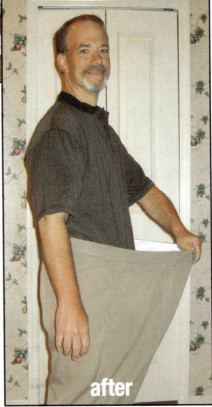

after

Another Success Story

Michelle is now a size 10, after losing **117** pounds!

Another Success Story

Chris - before

Chris - Crossing the Finish Line

REFERENCES

Hewitt, P.L. & Flett, G. (2004). Multidimensional Perfectionism Scale (MPS), Technical Manual. Tonawanda, NY: Multi-Health Systems, Inc.

Kubler-Ross, E. (1969). On Death and Dying. New York: Macmillian.

Park, M. (2010, November 8). Twinkie diet helps nutrition professor lose 27 pounds. CNN. Retrieved March 2011, from http://www.cnn.com/2010/HEALTH/11/08/twinkie.diet.professor/index.html.

Gearhardt AN, Grilo CM, DiLeone RJ, Brownell KD, Potenza MN. Can food be addictive? Public health and policy implications. Addiction. 2011 June; 106 (7): 1208-1212.

Gearhardt AN, Yokum S, Orr PT, Stice E, Corbin WR, Brownell KD. Neural correlates of food addiction. Archives of General Psychiatry. 2011 Apr: e1-e9.

Kenny, PJ, Johnson PM. Addiction-like reward dysfunction and compulsive eating in obese rats: Role for dopamine D2 receptors
Nature Neuroscience 13, 635–641 (2010)

David CW Lau, Hongyun Yan, Bikramjit Dhillon. Metabolic syndrome: A marker of patients at high cardiovascular risk
Can J Cardiol. 2006 February; 22(Suppl B): 85B–90B.

O'Brien PE, Dixon JB, Laparoscopic adjustable gastric banding in the treatment of morbid obesity. Archives of Surgery 2003;138(4): 376-82

Brethauer SA, Harris JL, Kroh M, Schauer PR. Laparoscopic gastric plication for treatment of severe obesity. Surg Obes Relat Dis. 2011 Jan-Feb; 7(1): 15-22. Epub 2010 Nov 9.

TESTIMONIALS

Dr. Aguila brings a unique perspective to the battle of the bulge as both a patient struggling with weight control through the trials and tribulation of life and as a medical and surgical expert in the field of bariatric. Through his "Cycle of Obesity" blueprint, you'll learn that there are no magic pills or quick fixes to weight management, but there are answers, you just need to know the questions. Dr. Aguila's "Cycle of Obesity" helps you understand these key questions, so you can finally find the answer to long-term success.

~**Kevin D. Huffman, DO**, President and Founder of the American Bariatric Consultants

As a health writer, I've read countless books on how to lose weight. "Why I Don't Lose Weight" is the best I've seen. Dr. Aguila gets to the heart of the struggle with obesity, then gives practical solutions for overcoming that struggle and losing weight – for good. The fact he learned these lessons through his own obesity problem makes his book even more compelling.

~Susan Hemmingway, Freelance health writer

Another example of how it is the individual who has the power to reverse their health conditions by first accepting responsibility, taking a real look at themselves inside and out, and committing to lifetime changes that are appropriate for them. Wonderfully clear and simple steps to permanent better health from a physician who has lived it.

~**Connie Gee, VP**, Healthcare Data Analyst and Wellness Strategist for Med-Vision, LLC

Dr. Aguila support classes have changed my life and the way I think about food. I am a new man, I have lost upwards of 70 pounds and I am committed to keep the weight off. The biggest thing it has given me is not only the confidence to change my eating habits and loose weight, but it has changed the way I view myself now, and that has opened the door to many others things in my life. It has helped me to break a cycle of the way I look at myself in a negative light. No pills, no schemes, just reprogramming the way you eat, not letting the food take you over. I feel great, like can achieve anything. I have been going back to school now for two years, working on my Associates degree in Business. Dr. aguila has helped me to reprogram the way I think about food and it changed my life in many ways. The journey will be life changing. It has changed my life and it will change yours too.

~**James B.**, Patient

I would like to say thanks to Dr. Aguila and staff for all that they have done for me and my wife. I was the world class skeptic when it came to ways to losing weight and have been to several seminars on weight loss. But when I talked with Dr. Aguila and saw exactly what to expect, I felt that this was the answer I was looking for. Dr. Aguila tells us what things could be done and how to deal with not just guilt, but relating obesity with the grief syndrome and how stress can effect a persons way to lose weight. I could go on and on but I know this really does work. It is just that simple! In 2 years I have lost 160 lbs. and have my life back. Thanks Dr. Aguila.

~**James G.**, A very satisfied patient

Endorsements of **Dr. A** and "Why I Don't **Lose Weight!**"

"Why I Don't Lose Weight! is a refreshing and original look at the root causes that keep you trapped in an emotional eating cycle. I recommend this book to anyone who is struggling with his or her weight."
– John Gray, PhD, #1 New York Times bestselling author of Men are from Mars, Women are from Venus

"Dr. Aguila's book, Why I Don't Lose Weight, offers a heart-felt, compassionate approach to understanding weight loss. This is not a diet book or a book of quick fixes. Instead it shows you practical ways to change from the inside out."
- Marci Shimoff, #1 NY Times bestselling author of "Love for No Reason and Happy for No Reason," co-author of "Chicken Soup for the Woman's Soul."

"Dr. A does a fantastic job of explaining how the Cycle of Obesity keeps you trapped and, more importantly, he helps you get out of it!"
- Dr. Mike Dow, Author of "Diet Rehab" and Co-Host of TLC's Freaky Eaters.

"Why I Don't Lose Weight!" is spot on! In it, Dr. A uncovers the real reasons why obesity seems so hard to cure. This book treats the cause, not the symptoms, empowering readers to lose the weight, and more important, to keep it off for good!"
- Max Bolka, Co-Author: Success is a State of Mind Co-Star: The Keeper of the Keys.

Why I Don't Lose Weight!

WILFRED AGUILA M.D., F.A.C.S.

Bookmarks Publishing is pleased to announce additional titles by Dr. A coming in 2012 including "The Seven Stages of Weight Loss, from Couch Potato to Fit and Healthy" and "UNBEATABLE, How You Can Obtain Success in Life, Love and Business."

-- Bookmarks Publishing, *mark a new chapter in your life.*